WORK PERMITS AND VISAS

1996

Jacqueline R. Bart
B.A., LL.B., J.D.

Benjamin J. Trister
LL.B., J.D.

CARSWELL
Thomson Professional Publishing

Canadian Cataloguing in Publication Data

Bart, Jacqueline R., 1967-
    Work permits and visas

(Carswell practice guides.   Immigration series)
Includes index.
ISBN 0-459-56038-7

1.   Visitors, Foreign — Legal status, laws, etc. —
Canada.   2. Alien labor — Legal status, laws, etc. —
Canada.   3. Visas — Canada.   I. Trister, Benjamin
J., 1960-   . II. Title. III. Series.

KE4454.B37 1995   342.71'082   C95-933146-8
KF4819.B37 1995

CARSWELL
Thomson Professional Publishing

One Corporate Plaza, 2075 Kennedy Road, Scarborough, Ontario M1T 3V4
Customer Service:
Toronto 1-416-609-3800
Elsewhere in Canada/U.S. 1-800-387-5164
Fax 1-416-298-5094

Acknowledgments

There are many people who have indirectly assisted me in the writing of this book including my parents, Jack and Margaret Bart, my sisters, Pamela Bart and Cynthia Kelly, and my Paralegal Assistant, Cammy Tam. I am also grateful to my Associates, Andrea White and Thomas G. Sosa for their support.

This project would not have been possible without the diligence of our editor and friend, Julia Gulej.

This book is dedicated in the loving memory of my grandmother Alberta Groot, who was deceased on July 20, 1995.

Jacqueline R. Bart

I wish to express my gratitude to Nan Berezowski of Greenberg Trister Turner for her co-authorship of the chapters on the North American Free Trade Agreement and the General Agreement on Trade in Services. I would also offer my thanks to Howard D. Greenberg for his assistance in the preparation of the chapter on the GATS.

Others, without whose patience and support this text would not exist, include Amalia, William and Rachel Trister.

Benjamin J. Trister

Summary Table of Contents

For a detailed Table of Contents, see page vii

Table of Contents

Chapter 3
TEMPORARY ENTRY TO CANADA

Chapter 5
THE GENERAL AGREEMENT ON TRADE IN SERVICES

Chapter 6
EMPLOYMENT AUTHORIZATIONS

Chapter 7
TEMPORARY ENTRY INTO CANADA:
EMPLOYMENT VALIDATIONS

Chapter 8
MISCELLANEOUS ISSUES ARISING FROM THE MIGRATION
OF A FOREIGN WORKER TO CANADA

Introduction

The practice of Immigration law is an art. The rules are difficult to find and are often not applied as written. Immigration is, above all, a human process, and immigration officers are given a relatively wide ambit of discretion. It is therefore, not uncommon for the success of an application to depend on the talents of the applicant's immigration counsel and the judgment of the particular immigration officer determining the merits of the application.

In this book, the authors endeavour to provide practitioners with a range of issues relating to successful visitor and foreign worker entry into Canada. These issues include the selection of the proper category for qualification for employment authorization such as visa requirements, medical requirements, criminal inadmissibility, employment law considerations, customs law issues, taxation and pension issues, spousal employment, health coverage, and the ability of accompanying dependants of foreign workers to engage in studies in Canada. All of these issues are discussed to varying degrees in this book.

The authors' goal in writing this book is that immigration law practitioners will have a better understanding of the multitude of issues and judgment calls that they will face in each application submitted on behalf of visitors and temporary foreign workers.

1

THE REGULATORY PROCESS FOR TEMPORARY ENTRY TO CANADA

1.1 VISITORS

- A substantial portion of this book deals with entry into Canada of individuals who seek to enter Canada temporarily for a purpose other than to enter the Canadian labour market. These would include:

  ○ tourists,

  ○ temporary foreign students, and

  ○ business people seeking to enter Canada to consult with counterparts at a Canadian company related to their foreign employer.

- Depending on the applicant's citizenship and immigration status elsewhere, a visitor visa may or may not be required.

- The applicant is expected to meet Canada's medical and criminal inadmissibility requirements although the degree of scrutiny of the applicant in relation to these requirements often depends on her or his country of origin.

- Certain foreign workers are exempt from the requirement to obtain employment authorizations. These individuals most often fall within the exemption stated in:

  ○ section 19 of the *Immigration Regulations*;

  ○ the business visitor provisions of the North American Free Trade Agreement ("NAFTA"); and º the business visitor provisions of the General Agreement on Trade in Services ("GATS").

Typically, the entry of persons engaged in these activities would not have an adverse impact on the local labour market.

1.2 FOREIGN WORKERS REQUIRING TEMPORARY EMPLOYMENT AUTHORIZATIONS

- A temporary foreign worker who seeks to enter the Canadian labour market is most often required to obtain permission in the form of an employment authorization.

- When the applicant and her or his employer seeks information from the government of Canada on how to proceed with an application for employment authorization, in most cases they are directed to the Canada Employment Centre to begin the application process. *For reasons which will be discussed later in this text, this is very often not the most expedient or practical procedure to follow.*

- Those who are experienced with Canada's system for admission of visitors and temporary foreign workers are well aware that the system has evolved to one which is governed by exemptions to the government's primary regulations relating to such admission. *The specifics of these exemptions are often set out in policies, some of which are unwritten and are handed down from officer to officer, much like myths are handed down from generation to generation.*[1]

The underlying premise in the development of restrictions governing the movement of temporary workers to Canada is the "Canadians First" policy. Accordingly, the

---

1   An example of this is the Code E01 job validation exemption applicable to individuals who are seeking an employment authorization to establish a business for which Canadians will be recruited or trained. Many officers will refuse to extend such an employment authorization arguing that such status may be valid for only one year, after which the foreign worker must leave Canada. This policy is not derived from the *Act*, *Regulations* or manuals.

selection criteria relating to temporary entry to Canada were designed to provide comprehensive protection to the Canadian labour market, while providing for exceptions in cases where overriding policy considerations necessitated the subordination of ''labour market protection'' to a secondary consideration.

The implementation of this labour market strategy is best appreciated through a consideration of the following:

1) the legislative and policy framework governing the movement of personnel to Canada; and

2) administrative interpretation adopted by governmental officials who are empowered under the legislative and policy framework.

By examining both the legislative and administrative requirements, readers should gain an appreciation of the process and strategic considerations relating to the temporary entry of persons to Canada. This book discusses Canada's legislative and administrative requirements applicable to foreign workers and certain students, regardless of their country of origin, as well as the visitor and foreign worker provisions of the NAFTA and the GATS.

The *Immigration Regulations (Regulations)*, enacted pursuant to the *Immigration Act (Act)*, set forth the mechanism for controlling the movement of visitors and foreign workers to Canada.

- The general rule contained in the legislative provisions is that no person, other than a Canadian citizen or permanent resident, shall engage or continue in employment without a valid and subsisting employment authorization, the issuance of which is preceded by validation of the applicant's job offer by the Canada Employment Centre.

- An immigration officer shall not issue an employment authorization to a person if, in the officer's opinion, the employment of such a person will adversely affect the employment opportunities for Canadian citizens or permanent residents (subsection 20(1) of the *Regulations*).

  ○ In making this determination, the immigration officer shall consider:

    (a) the qualifications and experience of the foreign worker for the particular position in question;

(b) whether the employer has made reasonable efforts to hire Canadian citizens or permanent residents; and

(c) whether the working conditions and wages of the position offered are sufficient to attract and retain Canadian citizens or permanent residents (subsection 20(3)).

○ These latter two considerations are satisfied by the validation of the employer's job offer by the Canada Employment Centre situated in the geographic location where the employer carries on business.

- In many instances, individuals may be required to obtain an employment authorization but are exempt from the requirement to first obtain the validation from the Canada Employment Centre. These individuals most often fall within the provisions of section 20(5) of the *Regulations* or the non-business visitor provisions of the NAFTA and GATS.

- As readers will discover, the exemptions to the requirement to obtain employment authorizations and/or job validations are applicable so frequently so as to create a system which is more often governed by the exemptions rather than the rule.

- In effect, this reverses the order of analysis in the system. Instead of the Canada Employment Centre being the first office consulted in connection with the admission of a temporary foreign worker, the Canada Employment Centre is approached only if the exemptions are not applicable.

- For reasons stated later in this book, the Canada Employment Centre validation process is to be avoided where possible because the procedure to obtain a job validation entails significant cost and time delays to the procedure.

- Attached hereto as Appendix 1-A to this chapter is a flow chart which sets out the system as it should be applied to the admission of a temporary foreign worker. It should be noted that the Canada Employment Centre validation process appears only at the bottom of the chart after all other options have been exhausted.

This chart has been designed to provide readers with an overview of the book. The selection criteria set out in each chapter provide an explanation for each of the stages set out in the flow chart. In order to ensure a thorough understanding of the "Temporary Entry Chart", it is recommended that this book be read in its entirety.

1.3 SUMMARY

As noted above, the key to successful temporary migration to Canada is the development of a strategy which takes into account the relationship between the regulatory process and the administrative policies which govern the entry of visitors and foreign workers to Canada.

- Lawyers acting on behalf of an employer or a foreign worker must initially distinguish between those situations where entry to Canada is permitted without first obtaining an employment authorization and employment activities which require an employment authorization.

- Where an employment authorization is required, the task is then to apply the regulatory and policy considerations to determine whether or not validation is a necessary and appropriate procedure to pursue.

Immigration counsel must remain sensitive to the fact that immigration is a highly personal matter. While the personal aspect can be highly rewarding, unfortunately delays or refusals can be extremely distressing to the applicants. Immigration counsel who are in possession of a proper understanding of the regulations and policies affecting foreign workers, as well as the creativity necessary to apply these rules and regulations effectively, will very often earn lasting friendships with clients that they have been privileged to assist. The information provided in this book has been designed to maximize the success of immigration counsel acting on behalf of persons seeking temporary entry to Canada.

Appendix 1-A

Temporary Entry Chart

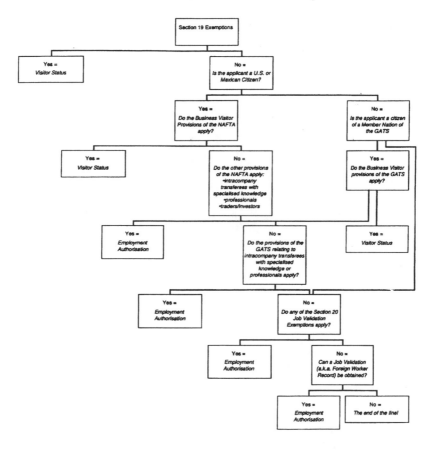

Section 19 Exemptions

Yes =
Visitor Status

No =
Is the applicant a U.S. or Mexican Citizen?

Yes =
Do the Business Visitor Provisions of the NAFTA apply?

No =
Is the applicant a citizen of a Member Nation of the GATS

Yes =
Visitor Status

No =
Do the other provisions of the NAFTA apply:
-intracompany transferees with specialised knowledge
-professionals
-traders/investors

Yes =
Do the Business Visitor provisions of the GATS apply?

Yes =
Employment Authorisation

No =
Do the provisions of the GATS relating to intracompany transferees with specialised knowledge or professionals apply?

Yes =
Visitor Status

Yes =
Employment Authorisation

No =
Do any of the Section 20 Job Validation Exemptions apply?

Yes =
Employment Authorisation

No =
Can a Job Validation (a.k.a. Foreign Worker Record) be obtained?

Yes =
Employment Authorisation

No =
The end of the line!

2

VISITOR VISAS

2.1 INTRODUCTION

Persons from a number of countries are required to obtain a visitor visa prior to making entry into Canada. Possession of a visitor visa, however, does not necessarily mean that holders are entitled to enter Canada as visitors. It is simply an indication of pre-approval for entry to Canada at a processing post abroad. The ultimate decision relating to the entry of visa holders to Canada is the responsibility of port-of-entry immigration officers.

- A visitor visa must be obtained at a Canadian visa office (i.e., high commission, embassy or consulate) outside Canada.

- Persons who may be required to obtain visitor visas prior to seeking entry to Canada include:

  ° visitors,

  ° foreign students, or

  ° foreign workers.

  A person who enters into Canada for the purpose of work or study will be required to obtain a visitor visa unless she or he is exempt under the Regulations.

- A visitor visa will not be required by a person seeking entry to Canada who is in possession of an Immigrant Visa and/or Record of Landing.

2.1.1 VISITOR VISAS DEFINED

The term "visitor visa" is not defined in the *Immigration Act* (*Act*) or the *Immigration Regulations* (*Regulations*). A "visa", however, "means a document issued or a stamp impression made on a document by a visa officer'' pursuant to section 2 of the *Act*. A ''visa officer'' means an immigration officer stationed outside Canada and authorized by order of the Minister to issue visas pursuant to section 2 of the *Act*.

- A visitor visa must be obtained prior to appearing at a Canadian port of entry and is a document evidencing that the holder meets the requirements of the *Act* and *Regulations*.

  The purpose of requiring a visitor visa is to prevent the entry of a person to Canada who does not qualify for permanent residence and who cannot or will not leave Canada.

- In accordance with section 13(2) of the *Regulations* the applicant is required to satisfy that she or he will be able to:

  ° return to the country from which she or he seeks to come to Canada; or

  ° go from Canada to some other country.

2.1.2 DEFINITION OF A VISITOR

Section 2 of the *Act* defines a ''visitor'' as:

> . . . a person who is lawfully in Canada, or seeks to come into Canada for a temporary purpose, other than a person who is
> (a) a Canadian citizen,
> (b) a permanent resident,
> (c) a person in possession of a permit, or
> (d) an immigrant authorized to come into Canada pursuant to paragraph 14(2)(b), 23(1)(b) or 32(3)(b).

- Anyone who is lawfully in Canada for a temporary purpose, i.e., whether tourism, business, employment or education, and who is not a Canadian citizen, permanent resident, permit holder or authorized pursuant to the paragraphs enumerated in the above-noted definition, is considered a "visitor".

''A person in possession of a permit'' means someone who is in possession of a permit issued under subsection 37(1) (i.e. a ministers's permit) pursuant to the definition of ''permit'' which is set out in section 2(1) of the *Regulations*.

The use of the word ''permit'' does not relate to a student or employment authorization. All individuals entering Canada under a visitor, student or employment authorization are considered visitors during their stay in Canada.

- Both foreign students and persons entering Canada under the authority of an employment authorization will be required to obtain a visitor visa prior to entry to Canada (unless they are exempted) in the same manner as an individual who requests temporary entry to Canada for what would normally be considered a business or pleasure visit to Canada (i.e., "visitor" activities such as tourism or meetings) (section 13 of the *Regulations*).

- Visitor status must be obtained by anyone entering Canada as a tourist under:

  ° the exemptions to the requirement to obtain an employment or student authorization (sections14 or 19(1) of *Regulations*); or

  ° the authority of an employment or student authorization or Minister's Permit.

- A visitor visa is a document which provides a person, who by law is required to obtain a visitor visa, with the opportunity to apply for visitor status in Canada at a Canadian port of entry. Without possession of a visitor visa, such an individual would not be able to apply for visitor status or an employment or student authorization.

- If a visitor visa is required, the visa is a prerequisite to obtaining visitor status or an employment or student authorization.

- Often a person who applies for a visitor visa at a processing post, will simultaneously apply for visitor status in one of the authorized visitor categories under the *Act* and *Regulations*.

2.2 PERSONS REQUIRED TO OBTAIN A VISITOR VISA

Not everyone is required to obtain a visitor visa prior to appearing at a port of entry. Section 9(1) of the *Act* states that all visitors must obtain a visitor visa except in prescribed cases. Section 13(1) of the *Regulations* states that all persons, except those appearing in Schedule II to the *Regulations* are required to obtain visitor visas.

At this time, *inter alia*, citizens of the following countries do not need a visitor visa in order to appear at a Canadian port of entry:

Andorra, Austria, Belgium, Costa Rica, Dominica, Germany, Iceland, Italy, Liechtenstein, Malta, Namibia, New Zealand, St. Kitts & Nevis, San Marino, Solomon Islands, Sweden, United Kingdom, Venezuela, Antigua & Barbuda, Bahamas, Botswana, Cyprus, Finland, Greece, Ireland, Japan, Luxembourg, Mexico, Nauru, Norway, St. Lucia, Saudi Arabia, Spain, Switzerland, United States, Western Samoa, Australia, Barbados, Brunei, Denmark, France, Grenada, Israel, Kiribati, Malaysia, Monaco, Netherlands, Papua New Guinea, St. Vincent, Singapore, Swaziland, Tuvalu, Vanuatu and Zimbabwe.

Attached as Appendix 2-A is a List of Countries Whose Citizens Require Visitor Visas.

The Federal Court of Appeal has held that section 13(1) of the *Regulations* and Schedule II of the *Regulations* is not discriminatory and, accordingly, does not infringe on the *Canadian Charter of Rights and Freedoms* (see *Okadia v. Min. of Employment & Immigration* (1983), 5 D.L.R. (4th) 187 (Fed. C.A.).

2.3 APPLICATION PROCEDURE FOR PERSONS REQUIRING A VISITOR VISA

2.3.1 PROCESSING POST OUTSIDE OF CANADA

- A persons who is required to obtain a visitor visa must make an application for a visitor visa at a processing post outside of Canada.

- Counsel must ensure that the client is able to obtain entry to the country hosting the Canadian processing post; otherwise, the client may not be in a position to attend an interview if required, thereby preventing the completion of the processing of her or his application for a visitor visa, which may ultimately result in the refusal of the application.

2.3.2 APPLICATION TO BE ASSESSED BY A VISA OFFICER

It is the responsibility of the visa officer to assess applications in order to determine whether applicants and their dependants are persons to whom entry to Canada may be granted (section 9(2.1) of the *Act*). The visa officer is required to assess all persons seeking entry to Canada, including foreign students and foreign workers.

- Visa officers have been granted substantial discretion under the *Act*. An officer may issue a visa if she or he is satisfied that the person seeking entry to Canada meets the criteria set out in the *Act* and *Regulations* (section 9(4) of the Act).

2.3.3 REQUIREMENT OF TEMPORARINESS

- Applications for visitor visas are assessed on the basis of the ability of the person, subsequent to entry, to leave Canada and return to her or his country of citizenship or another country (section 13 of the *Regulations*).

- Visa officers require that tourists, business visitors, foreign students and foreign workers demonstrate that their stay in Canada is temporary and that they do not intend to reside in Canada for an indeterminate period of time.

- Visa officers assess an application on the basis of the legal presumption that the applicant intends to remain in Canada permanently and it is the applicant's responsibility to demonstrate the temporariness of her or his stay in Canada as well as her or his right to come into Canada (section 8(1) & (2) of the *Act*). *In recent years, it has become the accepted practice at certain Canadian visa offices to relax this criteria for businesspeople and their dependants, whose presence in Canada is required prior to their being able to be processed for permanent residence status.*

2.3.4 REQUIREMENT TO SATISFY THE IMMIGRATION OFFICER OF NON-IMMIGRANT INTENT

- The onus is on the visa applicant to satisfy the immigration officer that she or he does not intend to emigrate to Canada (section 9(1.2) of the *Act*). *Accordingly, a person who intends to enter Canada temporarily, and possibly, permanently, depending on the success of her or his employment in Canada, is faced with an uncomfortable situation. This issue is addressed in further detail under the section headed "Dual Intention" below.*

2.3.5 THE REQUIREMENT OF TRUTHFULNESS

- It is the duty of each person applying for a visitor visa to answer truthfully all questions put to her or him by an immigration officer for purposes of assessing whether the applicant is admissible (section 9(3) of the *Act*). *An applicant who does not answer questions truthfully may be inadmissible to Canada as she or he may come within the provisions of section 19(2)(d) of the Act. A violation of section 9(3) of the Act may, but does not automatically, mean that the applicant is inadmissible to Canada. (Kang v. Min. of Employment and Immigration, [1981] 2 F.C. 807 (Fed. C.A.))*

Misleading statements are statements that: are false *and* made with the intention to mislead (whether written or oral); and relate to the admissibility of the applicants or their dependants.

The requirement of truthfulness impacts upon the credibility of the applicants. If applicants utter untrue statements in relation to matters pertaining to their temporary entry to Canada, the credibility of their entire application is affected. Issues of credibility and truthfulness are issues that visa officers are required to assess.

In order for a court to reverse a decision of a visa officer based on the credibility of the applicant, there must be an error of law apparent on the face of the record or a breach of the duty of fairness.

2.3.6 REQUIREMENT TO PROVIDE DOCUMENTATION REQUESTED BY IMMIGRATION OFFICER

- Visa officers may require that the applicant provide substantiating documentation (section 9(3) of the *Act*).

- Section 1.06(2) of the *Immigration Manual* restricts the type of documentation which may be requested to ". . . evidence to confirm identity, family relationship, character, education, occupation, or other claims relating to [the applicant's] admission."

2.3.7 REQUIREMENT THAT THE VISA OFFICER BE SATISFIED THAT THE APPLICANT'S ENTRY WOULD NOT BE CONTRARY TO THE *ACT* OR *REGULATIONS*

Applicants will be refused a visitor visa if they are inadmissible to Canada pursuant to the *Act* or *Regulations* (section 9(4) and (5) of the *Act*).

- Persons who are inadmissible to Canada are listed in section 19 of the *Act* and include, *inter alia*:

  ° persons likely to cause excessive demands on health and social services;

  ° persons who cannot or are unwilling to support themselves;

  ° persons convicted of offences which are punishable by a maximum of up to ten years in prison or more (whether offence was committed inside or outside Canada);

  ° persons who are members of an organization engaged in criminal activities;

  ° persons whom there are reasonable grounds to believe will commit an offence punishable by indictment or will engage in espionage, subversion, terrorism or activities

17

which would endanger the lives and safety of persons in Canada.

2.4 TYPES OF VISITOR VISAS

There are a number of types of visitor visas in addition to regular visitor visas. These include:

1. diplomatic and official visas

2. courtesy visas

3. transit visas and

4. collective certificates.

2.4.1 DIPLOMATIC AND OFFICIAL VISAS

- All Diplomats, consular officers and representatives or officials of a foreign country, of the United Nations or of international organizations (except persons holding diplomatic official, special or service passports from Turkey who come to Canada on postings) are required to apply for and obtain a visa before presenting themselves at a Canadian port of entry.

  - Different rules apply for U.S. government officials because they fall within item 12 of Schedule II of the *Regulations.*

- A visitor visa must also be obtained for the accompanying family members of diplomats, consular officials and representatives or officials of a foreign country, of the United Nations or of international organizations.

2.4.2 COURTESY VISAS

- Visa officers have the discretion to issue courtesy visas to persons who, although not entitled to diplomatic privileges and immunities as a result of their position or the purpose of their entry to Canada, are, nonetheless, considered sufficiently important so as to distinguish and facilitate their admission to Canada.

- Courtesy visas may be issued to persons from all nationalities whether they require visas or are visa exempt.

A courtesy visa provides notification to the immigration officer at the port of entry that the person they are dealing with is of exceptional merit or importance and is to be treated courteously and provided service in an expeditious manner. Otherwise, courtesy visa holders are subject to the normal requirements of the Act and the Regulations and courtesy visas do not exempt persons from regular examination procedures (see Immigration Manual, Chapter PE-6, page 6).

2.4.3 TRANSIT VISAS

- Transit visas are provided to individuals travelling to a third country who are required to make a brief stop in Canada.

- Instead of providing a transit visa, an immigration officer may provide a collective certificate which will be used by the group in lieu of individual transit visas.

2.4.4 COLLECTIVE CERTIFICATES

- Collective certificates may be issued by visa officers in two instances:

  o to groups visiting in the United States who wish to make a brief visit or tour of Canada and whose members require visitor visas; or

  o to groups in transit to destinations other than Canada by airfare when the aircraft is scheduled to refuel in Canada and the passengers require visitors visas.

If a visa officer believes that there is some enforcement risk in providing a collective certificate, she or he may require all individual group members to apply for visitor visas independently.

2.4.5 VISITOR VISAS

All references to visitor visas relate to persons who require a document prior to making entry to Canada because they are not citizens of the countries listed above in this chapter.

2.5 RIGHTS OF VISA HOLDERS

We note that possession of a visitor visa provides the holder with certain rights; however, it does not entitle the holder to enter Canada. In *Min. of Employment & Immigration v. Mercier* (September 16, 1980), Montreal Doc. No. 79-1243 (Imm. App. Bd) the Immigration Appeals Board held that a visitor visa issued outside of Canada gave the holder a ''colour of right'' to come into Canada as a visitor (or an immigrant, as the case may be) but no other rights other than the colour of right.

2.5.1 PRESUMPTION OF IMMIGRATION

Section 8(2) of the *Act* states that every person who seeks to come into Canada will be presumed to be an immigrant. The immigration officer is, therefore, required by law to assume that the person is an immigrant. An immigrant is defined in section 2 of the Act as ''. . . a person who seeks landing''. Furthermore, ''. . . landing means lawful permission to establish permanent residence in Canada''. Accordingly, the presumption is that the person seeking to come into Canada intends to live in Canada on a permanent basis.

- It is the responsibility of the applicant for visitor status to rebut this presumption.

- For the applicant seeking entry into Canada who requires a visitor visa, a bifurcate level of scrutiny applies, and the applicant is required to "pass" both stages:

  ○ The first stage is performed by visa officers abroad and it provides certain rights of appeal to the visa holder which would otherwise not be available.

° The second stage is the port-of-entry examination by an immigration officer.

For an expansive discussion of this bifurcate level of scrutiny see *Grewal v. Canada (Min. of Employment & Immigration)* (1989), 8 Imm. L.R. (2d) 100 (Fed. C.A.).

2.6 PROCEDURE FOR APPLYING FOR A VISITOR VISA

2.6.1 DOCUMENTATION REQUIRED

- In order to apply for a visitor visa, the person seeking entry to Canada is required to submit various documentation in support of her or his application.

(a) Application Form (Application For Temporary Entry into Canada) (Visitor Visa)

- The application form is the most important document which the applicant must submit to the processing post to commence the processing of a visitor visa request. *See Appendix 2-B for reproduction of a visitor visa application form.*

- An applicant must list both her or his present address as well as her or his permanent address on the application form. The reason for this request is that it is not unusual for a person to make an application in a country which is not her or his home country. *For example, the applicant may be working in the United States and may wish to enter Canada from the United States, but may be originally from India.*

- Counsel should list their office address as the mailing address in order to ensure receipt of all correspondence from the processing post. *Note, however, that many visa offices will not use counsel's mailing address particularly if counsel's address is not within the visa office's jurisdiction.*

21

- Any dependants accompanying the applicant to Canada must be listed at item 9 of the form.

  ○ Dependants are spouses and sons or daughters of the applicant or their spouse if the children are under the age of 19 and unmarried. *See section 2 of the* Regulations *for a broader definition of "dependant".*

- Generally, if the applicant leaves her or his family behind, this is favourable in relation to the success of the application, as the entry would appear to be consistent with a temporary stay as most applicants do not intend to abandon their spouses and/or children.

- State the purpose of the applicant's visit at item 11 of the application *(i.e., whether it is to attend a meeting, visit a friend or family member, enjoy a holiday, study or engage in employment).*

- State the applicant's occupation at item 12 of the application. Generally, an applicant who is considered to have an employment position outside of Canada to which she or he would apparently return to will receive more favourable treatment than an applicant who does not have gainful employment.

- Specific medical requirements apply to items 19 and 20. In the event that the applicant has lived in a country or area for six months that in the opinion of the Minister of Health has a higher incidence of serious communicable disease than Canada, during the five-year period preceding the application, the applicant may be required to undergo medical examinations. *Please make reference to section 2.8, infra.*

  ○ If an applicant will likely be required to undergo a medical examination, which may delay visa issuance by weeks or months, restrict the applicant's visit to a period of less than six months at items 14 and 16 in order to avoid the requirement of a medical examination if one is otherwise required.

Note, however, that in certain cases in which the visa officer does not believe that the applicant's stay will be for less than six months, or when an applicant comes from an area which has a high incidence of communicable diseases, the visa officer may nonetheless impose a medical requirement. Also note that it would be improper to state an initial period of six months merely to avoid the imposition of a medical requirement if it is known that the applicant will want to remain in Canada for more than six months.

- If additional time in Canada is required subsequent to entry, then an extension of the applicant's visitor status may be applied for inland.

• State whether multiple or single entries are required into Canada (item 15).

- If multiple entries into Canada are required, the request must appear clearly marked on the application form so that a multiple-entry visa may be provided to the applicant.

- Otherwise, only a single entry visa will be granted and a new visa application will normally have to be made for each subsequent entry into Canada.

• State the amount of funds that the applicant will have available during her or his stay in Canada (item 17). *The more funds available to the individual while in Canada, the more comfortable the officer will be with the entry of the individual given the fact that the possibility that the applicant will take advantage of Canadian Health and Social Services will be substantially reduced.*

• Some posts also require that the applicant complete additional questionnaires or a Supplementary Information Form.

(b) Valid and Current Passports or Recognized Travel Documents

- All visitors to Canada are required to be in possession of a current passport or travel document in order to obtain entry to Canada (section 14(3) of the *Regulations*). *The term "travel document" is nowhere defined in the Act or Regulations. However, the kinds of documents which are considered to be travel documents for purposes of this section are set out in section 14(1), (3) and (5) of the Regulations and Schedule VII of the Regulations.*

- Please refer to Appendix 2-C for a list of travel documents which are recognized by Canadian authorities.

(c) Passport Size Photographs

- This requirement varies depending on the processing post as well as the country of citizenship of the applicant (generally two passport size photographs are required).

(d) Valid U.S. Temporary Entry Permit (I-94) or in the Case of Students, I-20AB and in the Case of "J" Visa Holders, DSP-66 or IAP-66

- Applications of non-United States citizens or residents generated in the United States should be accompanied with proof that the applicant is legally permitted in the U.S. *If proof that the applicant is legally residing in the United States cannot be furnished, the application may be refused because the officer may be suspicious that the individual is not legally present in the U.S. As a result, the applicant may be considered to have failed to rebut the presumption that she or he is emigrating to Canada.*

(e) Evidence of return transportation

- Return airfare, train fare, etc.

(f) Evidence of Sufficient Funds

- Proof that the applicant possesses the funds set out on the application form should be submitted with the application form.

- Proof may be provided by way of bank letters, letters of employment which mention the applicant's salary, copies of bank records, travellers cheques, etc.

- In countries with currency restrictions or unusually high inflation rates, the officers may also require proof that there are funds located outside the country or letters from the relatives or the persons whom the applicant intends to visit, stating that they will assume financial responsibility for the applicant during sojourn to Canada.

- In the case of an applicant entering Canada for business, the company requiring the presence of the applicant, where applicable, may advise the processing post that it shall be responsible for all expenses in relation to the applicant's entry to Canada, including accommodation, transportation, *per diem* expenses, etc.

    The funds which the applicant intends to bring to Canada should be sufficient in order to maintain the applicant at a reasonable standard of living while in Canada. This determination is clearly subjective in nature. For example, a foreign student entering Canada may be required to demonstrate that she or he has sufficient funds in order to pay for food, lodging, tuition and miscellaneous expenses which may arise.

(g) Letter of Leave From Employer

- The application package should include a letter from the applicant's employer which serves to notify the processing post that the employer is aware that the applicant will be travelling to Canada and that the employment position of the applicant shall be available to the applicant upon her or his return from Canada. *In the case of a student visa applicant, a letter from an employer stating that the applicant will be returning to employment upon completion of the course of study is also helpful.*

- The letter should also specify the anticipated length of the leave of absence, holiday or business trip.

(h) Documentation From Canada Evidencing Purpose of Entry to Canada

- All applications for temporary entry should, as a general rule, be accompanied by documentation of a Canadian source, stating the purpose of the applicant's entry to Canada.

- If the applicant is attending school, evidence regarding acceptance and enrolment (schools generally provide foreign students with an immigration letter) will be required for the processing of her or his application.

  - Note, however, that an accompanying dependant of a temporary foreign worker may apply for a student authorization after arriving in Canada. In such a case, a letter from the school or school board will not be required. Although it is possible to obtain a student authorization inland under these circumstances, an applicant who is required to obtain a visitor visa must still do so prior to arriving at a Canadian port of entry.

- If an applicant is entering Canada to visit relatives or friends she or he should provide the processing post with a letter from a relative or friend indicating her or his immigration status in Canada, occupation or position, employer, salary and address in Canada. *In difficult cases, the sponsor should also provide information about her or his good character, community involvement, religious or charitable activities and, if available, letters of reference or support. A letter of support from a local member of parliament or other professional endorsing the Canadian as a respectable person can be helpful.*

- A business applicant should also submit a letter from the Canadian business or company explaining the reason for the applicant's visit to Canada *(e.g., meeting with Canadian investors to discuss viability of new investment fund, job interview, vice-president's annual meeting, meeting of directors, meeting of shareholders).*

  - The letter should describe something about the Canadian business or company which is indicative of the legitimacy of the company *(e.g., size of company, number of employees, annual growth, profits or sales, nature of business conducted, importance of company in the Canadian economy).*

  - The letter should be placed on company letterhead and signed by an authorized signing officer who can be available to receive a telephone call from immigration officials.

  - The letter in support of the application should also state:

    1. that the applicant will not be compensated by the company, in any manner whatsoever, during the applicant's stay in Canada; and

    2. where applicable, that the applicant does not possess property or have close relatives in Canada.

- The applicant may also provide a letter from her or his employer in the country in which the application for a visitor visa was made which specifies the employment relationship between the applicant seeking entry and her or his employer, including salary, position at the company, length of employment to date, length of employment contract, importance of the employee to the employer's operation abroad, and the requirement to have the employee return to the foreign company upon the termination of her or his temporary visit to Canada.

27

- The employer letter should corroborate the letter of invitation of the Canadian person or company in relation to the purpose of the applicant's entry to Canada.

  Not all the foregoing documentation is required when applying for a visitor visa. Counsel should make a determination of the documentation which is required based on the strength, merit and category of the application.

(i) Processing Fee

- The application will not be processed without the correct processing fee.

- Processing fees are paid by certified cheque or money order in Canadian funds to "The Receiver General for Canada".

- Some processing posts offer alternative payment options, such as paying an equivalent fee in local currency to the processing post directly rather than to the Receiver General for Canada.

(j) Certificates of Good Conduct

- A visa officer may also require that the applicant provide a certificate of no criminal record from the local police authorities.

2.6.2 THE VISITOR VISA INTERVIEW

Visa officers have discretionary authority to interview applicants and their dependants for the purpose of assessing their application (section 22.1(2) of the *Regulations*).

- The interview must occur at the visa office where the application was submitted, or alternatively, where specified by the visa officer (section 22.1 (3) (a) of *Regulations*).

2.7 PORT OF ENTRY DETERMINATION

2.7.1 APPEARANCE BEFORE IMMIGRATION OFFICER AT PORT OF ENTRY

Section 12 of the *Act* states that every person seeking to come into Canada is required to appear before an immigration officer (or if a senior immigration officer is involved, at a place designated by the senior immigration officer) in order to determine whether the person will be granted admission to Canada.

- Once the applicant is in possession of a visitor visa, she or he would request temporary entry to Canada at the port of entry, as a visitor or as a holder of an employment or student authorization or a Minister's Permit.

2.7.2 EXAMINATION BY THE IMMIGRATION OFFICER

- During the course of examination, the person seeking entry to Canada is required to answer all questions posed by the immigration officer truthfully (see section 12(4) of the *Act*).

  The examination may include a brief request to describe the purpose of entry, or may be a lengthy examination which requires adjournment or an order of detention, in cases where the immigration officer is highly suspicious of the applicant (see section 12(3) of the Act).

- Pursuant to the *Immigration Manual*, Chapter PE-6, at page 8, immigration officers are required to take the following steps in determining whether to grant entry to a visitor:

(a) consider the intentions of the visitor:

- what is the applicant going to do in Canada? Are the person's plans well thought out, or merely frivolous? (Remember that although not all persons visiting Canada will have well thought-out plans, they should at least know what they are going to be doing for the first couple of days)

- for how long is the request? Considering the applicant's situation in his or her home country, is the time requested reasonable?

- is the person's understanding of a temporary purpose in accordance with the definition of a visitor?

- what family, employment or other responsibilities and obligations has the person left behind, and how have they been discharged?

(b) determine whether the client has the means to support himself or herself, or whether someone else is willing to provide adequate support.

(c) assess the client's ability to leave Canada: does the applicant have the means either to return to their home country or to proceed onward to a third country?

- Immigration officers will consider whether the person is listed as one of the inadmissible classes in section 19 of the *Act* and whether the person meets medical requirements.

2.7.3 CORROBORATIVE EVIDENCE

- Immigration officers are vested with the authority to request supporting documentation required for the purpose of establishing whether the person will be allowed to enter Canada as a visitor (see section 12(4) of the *Act*). Therefore:

  o A visa holder seeking entry to Canada at a port of entry should carry documentation which corroborates her or his oral testimony in relation to the purpose of her or his visit to Canada.

  o Counsel should advise the client that copies of documentation provided at the time of submission of the application, such as a letter of invitation or a letter from the employer, should also be made available to the immigration officers at the port of entry if requested.

2.8 MEDICAL EXAMINATIONS

Every visitor of a prescribed class is required to undergo a medical examination by a medical officer (section 11(1) of the *Act*). A medical examination includes a mental examination, a physical examination and a medical assessment of records respecting the person (see section 11(3) of the *Act*).

- Every person who meets the following two conditions below is required to be in possession of a valid certificate of assessment indicating that she or he is not a member of a medically inadmissible class to Canada:

  - if the person's entry to Canada exceeds a period of six consecutive months including actual or proposed absences from Canada for periods of less than 14 days; and

  - if the person has resided or sojourned, anytime during the period of one year immediately preceding the date of seeking entry in an area that is considered according to the Minister of Health to have a higher incidence of serious communicable diseases than Canada.

- In the event that the applicant is seeking immediate entry to Canada for a period of more than six months, and does not have time to wait for the results of a lengthy medical examination, the applicant may wish to apply for entry for a period of six months and once in Canada, apply for an extension beyond the six month period. The applicant would be required to undergo the medical examination from within Canada prior to obtaining visitor status extension.

- See Appendix 2-D for a list of areas or countries that in the opinion of the Minister of Health have higher incidences of serious communicable diseases than Canada.

2.9 GRANTING ENTRY

2.9.1 DURATION OF VISIT

- Immigration and visa officers may approve entry for a period of up to six months; *although longer periods of time may be granted as in the case, for example, of a dependant family member of a temporary foreign worker whose employment authorization is valid for longer than six months.*

- Immigration officers are encouraged to grant entry for a period of six months even in the case where a person requests entry for a very brief period of time. *The policy reasoning forming the basis for this practice is that granting entry for a six month period of time precludes the need for the visitor to request an extension upon entry to Canada.*

- In some instances, an immigration officer will grant entry for a period of less than six months even if the applicant has requested entry for a full six month period of time.

  ○ Situations where an immigration officer may grant entry for a period of less than six months may include the following:

    1. where a person is in possession of a visitor visa indicating that the intended length of stay is for less than a period of six months;

    2. where a person's passport or travel document will expire before six months from the date of the person's arrival at a Canadian port of entry; or

    3. where a visitor is in transit through Canada.

- A visitor will be required to renew her or his status prior to expiry regardless of whether status expires on a weekend or statutory holiday. *If the applicant's status expires on a Saturday or Sunday but the individual does not report to an immigration office until the following Monday, she or he is reportable under section 27(2)(c) of the Act. See Parmar v. Min. of Manpower and Immigration, [1982] 1 F.C. 16 (Fed. T.D.).*

2.9.2 DOCUMENTING A VISITOR

- Generally, a visitor who enters Canada under the authority of a visitor visa, or who does not require a visitor visa, has her of his passport stamped or is verbally permitted entry to Canada.

- Sometimes a visitor shall be provided with a "visitor record", such as:

  ○ when the person seeking entry into Canada intends to remain in Canada longer than six months; or

  ○ at the discretion of the immigration officer, the visitor is documented for control purposes *(i.e., in the case of seamen, visitors entering Canada for medical treatment, persons extradited to Canada and who enter as visitors, or visitors on whom terms and conditions have been imposed).*

2.9.3 TERMS AND CONDITIONS ON VISITOR VISAS

- The terms and conditions that an immigration officer may impose on a visitor include the following:

  ○ length of time the visitor can remain in Canada;

  ○ prohibition against studying;

  ○ prohibition against working or a stipulation of the type of employment, the employer or the location or the period during which the visitor may engage or continue in employment;

  ○ area in which the visitor may travel while in Canada; and/or

  ○ the times and places at which the visitor is required to report for medical examinations, surveillance, treatment, or to furnish evidence in compliance of terms and conditions. *See section 23(3) of the* Regulations.

2.9.4 SECURITY DEPOSITS

- In situations where an immigration officer believes that a visitor may not comply with the terms and conditions imposed, the immigration officer is authorized to take cash deposits or bonds to ensure compliance with the terms and conditions (see section 18 of the *Act*).

- The Deputy Minister is authorized to forfeit the security deposit if the visitor fails to comply with any of the terms and conditions imposed.

- In the event that the visitor complies with the terms and conditions imposed, the sum of money or other security deposited will be returned to the visitor "as soon as practicable" (section 18(3) of the *Act*).

- The *Immigration Manual*, Chapter PE-6, page 16, provides guidelines to immigration officers in relation to situations which may warrant a recommendation that a bond be issued. These situations include the following:

  ○ if a person indicates an intention to enter as a visitor but, on examination, there is some concern that the person actually intends to remain in Canada permanently;

  ○ if the person presents himself or herself at the port of entry as a tourist but the immigration officer believes that the person's true intention is to work or study in Canada;

  ○ if the person informs the immigration officer that he or she originally sought entry to work or study in Canada but was not able to obtain the necessary authorization and is now entering as a tourist.

2.9.5 COUNSELLING

- An immigration officer is required under policy to provide information to a person who has queries relating to her or his grant of entry into Canada about:

  ○ the expiry date of the visit;

○ terms and conditions applied to her or his entry to Canada;

○ procedures for applying for an extension inland;

○ the cost involved in relation to an extension sought inside of Canada; and

○ information about cancellation or refund if she or he has been placed on a bond.

2.10 DUAL INTENTION

As noted earlier, one of the requirements of the *Act* in relation to the entry of visitors is the requirement of temporariness. Sometimes, however, a person enters Canada as a visitor, having already applied for permanent residence in Canada at a processing post abroad or within Canada. Although there appears to be no authority in the *Act* or *Regulations* for allowing entry of such persons, there is some case law which recognizes that a person may have the dual intent of immigrating as well as entering Canada on a temporary basis and leaving Canada in the event that they are not in receipt of their immigration status prior to the expiry of their visitor visa. The *Immigration Manual* clearly advises immigration officers to distinguish cases where persons enter Canada and intend to abide by immigration law in relation to temporary entry while simultaneously applying for permanent residence against cases where persons who have no intention of leaving Canada if their application for permanent residence is refused: *Bajwa v. Canada (Minister of Employment and Immigration)* (1987), 4 Imm. L.R. (2d) 300 (Imm. App. Bd.); *Swinton v. Canada (Minister of Employment and Immigration)* (1987), 4 Imm. L.R. (2d) 274 (Imm. App. Bd.); *Toor v. Canada (Minister of Employment and Immigration)* (1983), 144 D.L.R. (3d) 554 (Fed. C.A.); *Rajpaul v. Canada (Minister of Employment and Immigration).* [1987] 3 F.C. 257 (Fed. T.D.), varied [1988] 3 F.C. 157 (Fed. C.A.).

Furthermore, the Supreme Court of Canada refused leave on a decision by the Federal Court of Appeal in *Chan v. Canada (Minister of Manpower and Immigration)*, [1978] 1 F.C. 217 (Fed. C.A.) where it was concluded that the word "visitor" implied a specific limited duration in Canada and that a temporary entry under visitor status could not be for an indefinite period of time as the word temporary was not synonymous with an "indefinite" period. See also *Grewal v. Canada (Minister of Employment and Immigration)* (1988), 24 F.T.R. 126 (Fed. T.D.), reversed [1990] 1 F.C. 192 (Fed. C.A.).

However, notwithstanding *Chan v. Canada*, the Federal Court of Appeal has stated that persons applying for permanent residence in Canada and entering in the interim as visitors are not necessarily inadmissible unless they do not intend to return to their home country in the event that permanent residence is not granted.

- Provided that the immigration officer is convinced that the visitor will return to her or his country of origin at an unspecified period of time should the visitor not obtain permanent residence, entry will be granted.

- An applicant seeking a visitor visa to Canada pending determination of her or his application for permanent residence should clearly state that the entry is temporary (assuming, of course, that the applicant fully intends to depart Canada prior to the expiry of her or his visitor status). Otherwise, the immigration officer may presume immigration and will refuse entry.

2.11 REFUSING ENTRY

- An immigration officer has the discretion to refuse the entry of a visitor visa holder.

- The refusal of a visitor visa holder at a port of entry is reported to the post which issued the visitor visa in relation to the following details regarding the refusal:

    ° name and nationality of the subject of the A20(1) report;

    ° the person's date and place of birth;

    ° the visa number, date and office of issue;

    ° the date and port of entry where the person sought to enter Canada;

    ° reason for refusal, using the code letter for the reason for refusal:

        A = seeking permanent residence
        B = claims Convention refugee status
        C = intends to seek or take employment
        D = intends to follow a course of study

E = has insufficient funds to maintain himself or herself and dependants

F = medical inadmissibility

G = criminal inadmissibility

H = expired visitor's visa, and

I = other

- Aside from the foregoing, no other details ought to be provided to the visa office in the telex report unless the reason for the refusal is code "I".

2.12 RIGHT TO APPEAL FOR VISA HOLDERS

- A visa holder who is refused entry to Canada has the right of appeal from a removal order pursuant to section 70(2)(b) of the *Act.*

- No right of appeal exists for a person who was not in possession of a valid visitor visa when reported inadmissible.

2.13 APPLYING FOR AN EXTENSION OF VISITOR STATUS INLAND

- Once in Canada, a visa holder can obtain an extension of her or his visitor status by making an application to change or extend her or his status. Such an application is usually submitted by mail to the Case Processing Centre located in Vegreville, Alberta.

Appendix 2-A

Canadian Visitor Visa Exemptions

CITIZENS OF:

Andorra	Antigua & Barbuda	Australia
Austria	Bahamas	Barbados
Belgium	Botswana	Brunei
Costa Rica	Cyprus	Denmark
Dominica	Finland	France
Germany	Greece	Grenada
Iceland	Ireland	Israel
Italy	Japan	Kiribati
Liechtenstein	Luxembourg	Malaysia
Malta	Mexico	Monaco
Namibia	Nauru	Netherlands
New Zealand	Norway	Papua New Guinea
St. Kitts & Nevis	St. Lucia	St. Vincent
San Marino	Saudi Arabia	Singapore
Solomon Islands	Spain	Swaziland
Sweden	Switzerland	Tuvalu
United Kingdom	*United States*	Vanuatu
Venezuela	Western Somoa	Zimbabwe

United Kingdom: (1) British Citizens and British Overseas Citizens who are re-admissible to the United Kingdom.

(2) Citizens of British Dependent Territories, who derive their citizenship through birth, descent, registration, or naturalization in one of Anguilla, Bermuda, British Virgin Islands, Cayman Islands, Falkland Islands, Gibraltar, Hong Kong, Monserrat, Pitcairn, St.Helena, or Turks & Caicos Islands.

United States: (1) The citizens of Guam, Northern Mariana Islands, Puerto Rico, and the U.S. Virgin Islands are U.S. citizens and are therefore also visa exempt.

(2) The citizens of American Samoa and Palau are U.S. nationals and visa exempt.

(3) The citizens of the Marshall Islands and Micronesia are neither U.S. citizens nor U.S. nationals and therefore require visitor visas.

(4) Nationals and permanent residents of the U.S. are visa exempt.

Other Exemptions:
(1) Persons holding passports or travel documents issued by the Holy See (the Vatican).

(2) Members of a crew who seek entry for shore leave or an off-duty period, or for some other legitimate and temporary purpose, and persons who seek entry to become members of a crew, other than citizens of a foreign country with which the Government of Canada has entered into an agreement whereby such members of a crew or persons are required to obtain visas.

(3) Members of the armed forces of a country that is a designated state for the purposes of the Visiting Forces Act, who are seeking entry in order to carry out their official duties, other than persons who have been designated as civilian components of that force.

(4) Persons coming from the U.S. for an interview with a U.S. consular officer concerning a U.S. immigrant visa, where they are in possession of evidence satisfactory to an immigration officer that they will be granted re-entry to the U.S.

(5) Persons visiting Canada who, during that visit, also visit any contiguous territory and return to Canada therefrom, as visitors within the period authorized on their initial entry or any extension thereto.

(6) Persons in possession of valid and subsisting Canadian student authorizations or employment authorizations, seeking to return as visitors to Canada from any contiguous territory, where the authorizations were issued prior to the departure of those persons from Canada.

(7) Persons holding passports containing a valid and subsisting Diplomatic Acceptance, Consular Acceptance, or Official Acceptance stamp or visa issued by the Chief of Protocol for the Dept. of External Affairs on behalf of the Government of Canada.

(8) Persons holding valid and subsisting diplomatic, official, special, or service passports issued to them by a country with which Canada has entered into an agreement whereby each country is to exempt holders of such passports from the requirements to obtain visas.

COUNTRIES WHOSE CITIZENS REQUIRE VISITOR VISAS

Afghanistan**	Guatemala	Pacific-Islands-
Albania	Guinea	U.S. Trust Terr.
Algeria	Guinea-Bissau	Pakistan
Angola	Guyana	Panama
Argentina	Haiti	Paraguay
Armenia	Honduras	Peru
Azerbaijan	Hungary	Philippines
Bahrain	India	Poland
Bangladesh	Indonesia	Portugal
Belarus	Iran	Qatar
Belize	Iraq	Romania
Benin	Israel**	Russia
Bhutan	Ivory Coast	Rwanda
Bolivia	Jamaica	Saotome E Principe

Bosnia-Hercegovina	Jordan	Senegal
Brazil	Kazakhstan	Seychelles-The
Bulgaria	Kenya	Sierra Leone
Burkina-faso	Korea-North	Slovak Republic
Burundi	Korea-South	Slovenia
Cambodia	Kuwait	Somali
Cameroun	Kyrgyzstan	South Africa
Cape Verde	Laos	Sri Lanka
Cntrl African Rep	Latvia	Sudan
Chad	Lebanon	Surinam
Chile	Lesotho	Syria
China-People's Rep.	Liberia	Taiwan
Colombia	Libya	Tadjikistan
Comoros	Lithuania	Tanzania
Congo	Macedonia	Thailand
Croatia	Malagasy Rep.	Togo
Cuba	Malawi	Tongo
Czech-Republic	Maldives	Trinidad & Tobago
Djibouti	Mali	Tunisia
Dominican Rep.	Mauritania	Turkey
Ecuador	Mauritius	Turkmenistan
Egypt	Moldova	Uganda
El Salvador	Mongolia	Ukraine
Eritrea	Morocco	United Arab Emirates
Equatorial Guinea	Mozambique	Uruguay
Estonia	Muyanmar (Burma)	Uzbekistan
Ethiopia	Nepal	Vietnam
Fiji	Nicaragua	Yemen
Gabon	Niger	Yugoslavia
Gambia	Nigeria	Zaire
Georgia	Oman	Zambia
Ghana		

** Additional notes

Holders of laisser-passez, titres de-voyage or refugee travel documents require visas.

Re: Israeli passports: only Israeli citizens holding valid Israeli orange "travel document in lieu of national passport" require cvv. (Also: holders of Israel "brown passports" — they are not Israeli citizens and require a cvv. If it's a "blue passport" — they do not require cvv.)

A wait period may be involved for certain passport holders.

Some countries have "special visa instructions". Please refer to that list.

Appendix 2-B

Employment and Immigration Canada

◆ Employment and Immigration Canada   Emploi et Immigration Canada

File – Réf.	
Visa No. – Visa n°	
No. of Entries – Nombre d'entrées	
Until – Jusqu'au	
Length of Stay – Durée du séjour	
Issued on – Délivré le	
Officer – Agent	

**APPLICATION FOR
TEMPORARY ENTRY TO CANADA
(VISITOR STATUS)**

*DEMANDE D'AUTORISATION DE
SÉJOUR TEMPORAIRE AU CANADA
(STATUT DE VISITEUR)*

1. Surname (Family name) *Nom de famille*	First Name *Prénom*	Middle name *Autres prénoms*

2. Present address – *Adresse actuelle*	3. Address in home country – *Adresse dans le pays d'origine*
	☐ Same as in question 2 or *Préciser si elle diffère de celle donnée au 2*

Telephone number – Numéro de téléphone ▶

4. Date of Birth – *Date de naissance*			5. Place of Birth – *Lieu de naissance* City/Town – *Ville/Village*	Prov./State - *Prov./État*	Country - *Pays*	6. Citizen of *Citoyenneté*
D-J	M	Y-A				

7. Sex – *Sexe* ☐ Male *Homme* ☐ Female *Femme*   **8. Present marital status – *État civil*** ☐ Unmarried (never married) *Célibataire* ☐ Engaged *Fiancé(e)* ☐ Married *Marié(e)* ☐ Widowed *Veuf (Veuve)* ☐ Separated *Séparé(e)* ☐ Divorced *Divorcé(e)*

9. Personal details of family members who will accompany me to Canada
Renseignements sur les membres de ma famille qui m'accompagneront au Canada

	Family name *Nom de famille*	First and second names *Prénoms*	Date and place of birth *Date et lieu de naissance*	Relationship to me *Lien de parenté*	Citizenship *Citoyenneté*
b)					
c)					
d)					
e)					
f)					

10. Passport details for myself and for persons listed in question 9
Précisions portées sur le passeport – Visiteur et personnes mentionnées au 9

	First name *Prénom*	Passport number *N° du passeport*	Country of issue *Pays de délivrance*	Date of issue *Date de délivrance*	Date of expiry *Date d'expiration*
	Applicant *Requérant*				
a)					
b)					
c)					
d)					
e)					
f)					

IMM 1296 (05-90) 8

This form has been established by the Minister of Employment and Immigration
Formulaire etabli par le Ministre de l'Emploi et de l'Immigration

Canadä

11. The purpose of my visit to Canada is - *Objet de ma visite au Canada*	12. My present occupation is - *Profession actuelle*					

13. Name, address and relationship of any person(s) whom I will visit are - *Nom et adresse de toute personne à qui je rendrai visite et lien de parenté*

Name - *Nom*	Address in Canada - *Adresse au Canada*	Relationship to me - *Lien de parenté*

14. I intend to be in Canada between *J'ai l'intention de séjourner au Canada du*	▶	D-J	M	Y-A	and au ▶	D-J	M	Y-A

15. On this trip, I intend to leave and re-enter Canada
Pendant mon séjour, j'ai l'intention de quitter le Canada et d'y revenir   ▶   Times - *fois*

16. The approximate date of my final entry will be *La date approximative de ma dernière entrée au Canada est*	▶	D-J	M	Y-A

17. Funds available for my stay in Canada $ Cdn.
Je dispose, pour mon séjour, de $,*(en dollars canadiens)*

18. Have you or any member of your family ever: ("x" the appropriate box)
Les questions suivantes s'adressent également au visiteur et à tout membre de sa famille   *(Inscrire "x" dans la case appropriée)*

a) Been treated for any serious physical or mental disorders or any communicable or chronic diseases ?
Vous a-t-on jamais traité(e) pour une maladie mentale ou physique grave, ou pour une maladie contagieuse ou chronique ?   ☐ Yes / Oui   ☐ No / Non

b) Been convicted of any crime in any country ?
Vous a-t-on jamais trouvé(e) coupable d'un acte criminel dans quelque pays que ce soit ?   ☐ Yes / Oui   ☐ No / Non

c) Been refused admission to or ordered to leave Canada ?
Vous a-t-on jamais refusé l'admission au Canada ou enjoint de quitter le Canada ?   ☐ Yes / Oui   ☐ No / Non

d) Been refused a visa to travel to Canada ?
Vous a-t-on jamais refusé l'autorisation de séjour au Canada ?   ☐ Yes / Oui   ☐ No / Non

e) Obtained a Canadian Social Insurance Number ?
Vous a-t-on jamais attribué un numéro d'assurance sociale au Canada ?   ☐ Yes / Oui   ☐ No / Non

f) In periods of either peace or war, have you ever been involved in the commission of a war crime or crime against humanity, such as: willful killing, torture, attacks upon, enslavement, starvation or other inhumane acts committed against civilians or prisoners of war; or deportation of civilians ?
En période de paix ou de guerre, avez-vous déjà participé à la commission d'un crime de guerre ou d'un crime contre l'humanité, c'est-à-dire de tout acte inhumain commis contre des populations civiles ou des prisonniers de guerre, par exemple, l'assassinat, la torture, l'agression, la réduction en esclavage ou la privation de nourriture, etc., ou encore participé à la déportation de civils ?   ☐ Yes / Oui   ☐ No / Non

If the answer to any of the above is "yes", give details below – *Si vous avez répondu "oui" à l'une ou l'autre question ci-dessus, veuillez donner les précisions*

19. During the past five years have you or any family member accompanying you lived in any other country for more than six months ?
Au cours des derniers cinq ans, avez-vous vécu dans un autre pays pendant plus de six mois ? Ne pas oublier les membres de votre famille qui vous accompagneront au Canada   ▶   ☐ Yes / Oui   ☐ No / Non

20. If answer to question 19 is "yes" list countries and length of stay
Si la réponse au 19 est affirmative, indiquer le nom de ces pays et la durée du séjour

Country – *Pays*	Length of Stay *Durée du séjour*	Country – *Pays*	Length of Stay *Durée du séjour*

I declare that I have answered all required questions in this application fully and truthfully
Je déclare avoir donné des réponses exactes et complètes à toutes les questions de la présente demande

_____   _____
Signature of Applicant – *Signature du requérant*   Date

Appendix 2-C

Travel Documents

The *Immigration Regulations, 1978*, SOR/78-172 as amended provides:

14. (1) Subject to subsection (2), every immigrant shall be in possession of

(a) a valid and subsisting passport issued to that immigrant by the country of which he is a citizen or national, other than a diplomatic, official or other similar passport;

(b) a valid and subsisting travel document issued to that immigrant by the country of which he is a citizen or national;

(c) a valid and subsisting identity or travel document

(i) that was issued to that immigrant by a country, and

(ii) that is of the type issued to non-national residents of the country of issue, refugees, or stateless persons who are unable to obtain a passport or other travel document from their country of citizenship or nationality, or who have no country of citizenship or nationality; or

(d) a valid and subsisting identity or travel document issued to that immigrant and specified in item 1 of Schedule VII.

. . . . .

14. (3) Subject to subsection (4), every visitor shall be in possession of

(a) a valid and subsisting passport valid for travel to Canada, issued to that visitor by the country of which he is a citizen or national and recognised by the country of issue as giving that visitor the right to enter the country of issue;

(b) a valid and subsisting travel document issued to the visitor by the country of which he is a citizen or national and recognized by the country of issue as giving that visitor the right to enter the country of issue;

(c) a valid and subsisting identity or travel document that

(i) was issued to that visitor by a country,

(ii) is recognized by the country of issue as giving that visitor the right to enter the country of issue, and

(iii) is of the type issued to non-national residents of the country of issue, refugees or stateless persons who are unable to obtain a passport or other travel document from their country of citizenship or nationality, or who have no country of citizenship or nationality; or

(d) a valid and subsisting identity or travel document issued to that visitor and specified in item 2 of Schedule VII.

43

. . . . .

(5) A passport, identity or travel document specified in item 3 of Schedule VII is not a valid and subsisting passport, identity or travel document for the purposes of subsections (1) and (3).

SCHEDULE VII
(Section 14)

1. (1) A travel document issued by the International Committee of the Red Cross, Geneva, Switzerland, to enable and facilitate emigration.

(2) [Revoked SOR/90-605.]

(3) An exit visa issued by the Government of the Union of Soviet Socialist Republics to former citizens of that country compelled to relinquish their nationality in order to emigrate therefrom.

2. (1) A laissez-passer issued by the United Nations.

(2) [Revoked SOR/90-605.]

(3) A document issued by the Organization of American States entitled ''Official Travel Document''.

(4) A passport issued by the Government of the United Kingdom of a British Overseas Citizen.

3. (1) Any passport, identity or travel document purporting to be issued by Bophuthatswana, Ciskei, Transkei, or Venda.

(2) Any passport, identity or travel document purporting to be issued by the All Palestine Government.

(3) Any passport issued by the Government of the United Kingdom entitled 'British Visitor's Passport'.

Appendix 2-D

Country or area	Visitor medical required
Abu Dhabi *see* United Arab Emirates	
Admiralty Islands *see* Papua New Guinea	
Afghanistan	Yes
Agalega Island *see* Mauritius	
Ajman *see* United Arab Emirates	
Albania	Yes
Aldabra *see* Seychelles	
Aldernay *see* Great Britain	
Algeria	Yes
American Samoa	Yes
Amirantes *see* Seychelles	
Andorra	No
Anegada *see* British Virgin Islands	
Angola	Yes
Anguilla	Yes
Antigua and Barbuda	Yes
Argentina	Yes
Armenia	Yes
Aruba *see* Netherlands Antilles	
Ascension *see* St. Helena	
Assumption Island *see* Seychelles	
Austral Islands *see* French Polynesia	
Australia	No
Austria	No
Azerbaijan	Yes
Azores	Yes
Bahamas	No
Bahrain	Yes

Country or area	Visitor medical required
Balearic Islands *see* Spain	
Bangladesh	Yes
Barbados	Yes
Belarus	Yes
Belau *see* U.S. Trust Territory of the Pacific Islands	
Belgium	No
Belize	Yes
Benin	Yes
Bequia Island *see* St. Vincent and the Grenadines	
Bermuda	No
Bhutan	Yes
Bolivia	Yes
Bonaire *see* Netherlands Antilles	
Bophuthatswana *see* South Africa	
Bora Bora *see* French Polynesia	
Bosnia — Hercegovina *see* Yugoslavia	
Botswana	Yes
Brazil	Yes
Brechou *see* Great Britain	
British Indian Ocean Territory *see* Seychelles	
British Virgin Islands	Yes
Brunei	Yes
Bulgaria	Yes
Burkina Faso	Yes
Bruma *see* Myanmar	
Burundi	Yes
Cameroun	Yes
Canary Islands	Yes
Canouan Island *see* St. Vincent and the Grenadines	
Cape Verde	Yes
Carriacou Island *see* Grenada	

Country or area	Visitor medical required
Cayman Islands	Yes
Central African Republic	Yes
Chad	Yes
Chagos Archipelago *see* Seychelles	
Channel Islands *see* Great Britain	
Chile	Yes
China	Yes
Christmas Island *see* Australia	
Ciskei *see* South Africa	
Cocos Island *see* Australia	
Columbia	Yes
Comoros	Yes
Congo	Yes
Cook Islands *see* New Zealand	
Costa Rica	Yes
Croatia *see* Yugoslavia	
Crozet Archipalago *see* France	
Cuba	Yes
Curacao *see* Netherlands Antilles	
Cyprus	Yes
Czechsolovakia	Yes
Denmark	No
Desirade *see* Guadeloupe	
Desroches *see* Seychelles	
Djibouti	Yes
Dominica	Yes
Dominican Republic	Yes
Dubai *see* United Arab Emirates	
Easter Island *see* Chile	
Ecuador	Yes
Egypt	Yes

Country or area	Visitor medical required
El Salvador	Yes
England *see* Great Britain	
Equatorial Guinea	Yes
Estonia	Yes
Ethiopia	Yes
Falklands Islands	No
Farquhar *see* Seychelles	
Fiji	No
Finland	No
Formosa *see* Taiwan	
France	No
French Guiana	Yes
French Polynesia	Yes
Fujairah *see* United Arab Emirates	
Gabon	Yes
Gambia	Yes
Gambier Islands *see* French Polynesia	
Georgia	Yes
Germany	No
Ghana	Yes
Gibraltar	No
Great Britain	No
Greece	Yes
Greenland	No
Grenada	Yes
Guadeloupe	Yes
Guam	Yes
Guatemala	Yes
Guernsey *see* Great Britain	
Guinea	Yes
Guinea-Bissau	Yes

Country or area	Visitor medical required
Guyana	Yes
Haiti	Yes
Holy See	No
Honduras	Yes
Hong Kong	Yes
Huahine *see* French Polynesia	
Hungary	Yes
Iceland	No
India	Yes
Indonesia	Yes
Iran	Yes
Iraq	Yes
Ireland	No
Isle of Man *see* Great Britain	
Israel	No
Italy	No
Ivory Coast	Yes
Jamaica	Yes
Japan	No
Jersey *see* Great Britain	
Johnston Atoll *see* U.S. Trust Territory of the Pacific Islands	
Jordan except West Bank	Yes
Jordan, West Bank	Yes
Jost Van Dyke *see* British Virgin Islands	
Kampuchea	—
Kazakhstan	Yes
Kenya	Yes
Kerguelen Islands	Yes
Kiribati	—
Korea, North	Yes
Korea, South	Yes

Country or area	Visitor medical required
Kosrae *see* U.S. Trust Territory of the Pacific Islands	
Kuwait	Yes
Kyrgyzstan	Yes
Laos	Yes
Latvia	Yes
Lebanon	Yes
Les Saintes *see* Guadeloupe	
Lesotho	Yes
Liberia	Yes
Libay	Yes
Liechtenstein	No
Lithuania	Yes
Lord Howe Island *see* Australia	
Loyalty Islands *see* New Caledonia	
Luxembourg	No
Macao	Yes
Madeira	Yes
Maio *see* French Polynesia	
Makatea *see* French Polynesia	
Malagasy Republic	Yes
Malawi	Yes
Malaysia	Yes
Maldives	Yes
Mali	Yes
Malta	No
Marie Galante *see* Guadeloupe	
Marquesas Islands *see* French Polynesia	
Marshall Islands *see* U.S. Trust Territory of the Pacific Islands	
Martinique	Yes
Maupiti *see* French Polynesia	
Mauritania	Yes

Country or area	Visitor medical required
Mauritius	Yes
Mayotte	Yes
Mayreau *see* St. Vincent and the Grenadines	
Mexico	Yes
Micronesia *see* U.S. Trust of the Pacific Islands	
Midland Islands *see* U.S. Trust Territory of the Pacific Islands	
Moldova	Yes
Monaco	Yes
Mongolian People's Republic	Yes
Montserrat	Yes
Moorea *see* French Polynesia	
Morocco	Yes
Mozambique	Yes
Mustique *see* St. Vincent and the Grenadines	
Myanmar	Yes
Namibia	Yes
Nauru	Yes
Nepal	Yesm
Netherlands	No
Netherlands Antilles	Yes
Nevis *see* St. Kitts-Nevis	
New Britain *see* Papua New Guinea	
New Caledonia	Yes
New Guinea mainland *see* Papua New Guinea	
New Guinea Islands *see* Papua New Guinea	
New Ireland *see* Papua New Guinea	
New Zealand	No
Nicaragua	Yes
Niger	Yes
Nigeria	Yes
Nieu *see* New Zealand	

Country or area	Visitor medical required
Norfolk Island *see Australia*	
Northern Ireland *see* Great Britain	
Northern Mariana	Yes
Northern Sinai	Yes
Norway	No
Oman	Yes
Orkney Islands *see* Great Britain	
Pakistan	Yes
Palau *see* U.S. Trust Territory of the Pacific Islands	
Palestine *see* Israel	
Panama	Yes
Papua New Guinea	Yes
Paraguay	Yes
Peru	Yes
Philippines	Yes
Pitcairn Island *see* New Zealand	
Poland	Yes
Ponape *see* U.S. Trust Territory of the Pacific Islands	
Portugal	Yes
Puerto Rico	Yes
Qatar	Yes
Raiatea *see* French Polynesia	
Ras al Khaimah *see* United Arab Emirates	
Redonda *see* Antigua and Barbuda	
Reunion	Yes
Rodrigues *see* Mauritius	
Romania	Yes
Ronde *see* St. Vincent and the Grenadines	
Russia	Yes
Rwanda	Yes
Saba *see* Netherlands Antilles	

Country or area	Visitor medical required
Sabah *see* Malaysia	
Sark *see* Great Britain	
St. Barthelemy *see* Guadeloupe	
St. Brandon group *see* Mauritius	
St. Croix *see* U.S. Virgin Islands	
St. Eustatius *see* Netherlands Antilles	
St. Helena	Yes
St. John *see* U.S. Virgin Islands	
St. Kitts-Nevis	Yes
St. Lucia	Yes
St. Martin *see* Guadeloupe	
St. Maarten *see* Netherlands Antilles	
St. Pierre and Miquelon *see* France	
St. Thomas *see* U.S. Virgin Islands	
St. Vincent and the Grenadines	Yes
Saharawi Arab Democratic Republic	Yes
San Marino	No
Sao Tome and Principe	No
Sarawak *see* Malaysia	
Saudi Arabia	Yes
Scotland *see* Great Britain	
Senegal	Yes
Seychelles	Yes
Sharjah *see* United Arab Emirates	
Sierra Leone	Yes
Singapore	Yes
Slovenia *see* Yugoslavia	
Society Archipelago *see* French Polynesia	
Solomon Islands	Yes
Solomons, The	—
Somalia	Yes

Country or area	Visitor medical required
South Africa	Yes
Spain	No
Sri Lanka	Yes
Sudan	Yes
Suriname	Yes
Swaziland	Yes
Sweden	No
Switzerland	No
Syria	Yes
Tadjikistan	Yes
Tahaa *see* French Polynesia	
Tahiti *see* French Polynesia	
Taiwan	Yes
Tanzania	Yes
Terres Australes et antarctiques *see* France	
Thailand	Yes
Tibet *see* China	
Tobago Cays *see* St. Vincent and the Grenadines	
Togo	Yes
Tokelau *see* New Zealand	
Tonga	Yes
Tortola *see* British Virgin Islands	
Transkei *see* South Africa	
Trinidad and Tobago	Yes
Tristan da Cunha *see* St. Helena	
Truk *see* U.S. Trust Territory of the Pacific Islands	
Tuamotu Archipelago *see* French Polynesia	
Tunisia	Yes
Turkmenistan	Yes
Turkey	Yes
Turks and Caicos	Yes

Country or area	Visitor medical required
Tuvalu	Yes
Uganda	Yes
Ukraine	Yes
Umm al Qaiwain *see* United Arab Emirates	
United Arab Emirates	Yes
Union Island *see* St. Vincent and the Grenadines	
United States of America	No
Uruguay	Yes
U.S. Trust Territory of the Pacific Islands	Yes
U.S. Virgin Islands	Yes
Uzbekistan	Yes
Vanuatu	Yes
Vatican City State	No
Venezuela	Yes
Vietnam	Yes
Virgin Gorda *see* British Virgin Islands	
Virgin Islands *see* either British Virgin Islands or U.S. Virgin Islands, as applicable	
Wake Island *see* U.S. Trust Territory of the Pacific Islands	
Wales *see* Great Britain	
Wallis and Futuna	Yes
Western Samoa	Yes
Yap *see* U.S. Trust Territory of the Pacific Islands	
Yemem Arab Republic	Yes
Yemen, People's Demoractic Republic of	Yes
Yugoslavia	Yes
Zaire	Yes
Zambia	Yes
Zimbabwe	Yes

3

TEMPORARY ENTRY TO CANADA

3.1 TOURIST VISAS AND EXEMPTIONS TO STUDENT AND EMPLOYMENT AUTHORIZATIONS

Visitor status must be considered independently from visitor visas. Visitor status relates to the various visitor, employment and student authorization categories, as well as the exemptions to the requirement to obtain employment or student authorization.

- Persons qualifying for visitor status are applicants seeking entry into Canada as visitors who may qualify as tourists or under one of the exemptions to the requirement to obtain an employment or student authorization under the *Immigration Act* (*Act*) or *Immigration Regulations* (*Regulations*).

- The only guide available to immigration officers in relation to visitor activities are the exemptions from the requirement to obtain an employment authorization.

  ○ These exemptions may be found in the *Regulations*, the North American Free Trade Agreements ("NAFTA") and the General Agreement on Trade in Services ("GATS").

  ○ Immigration officials provide entry to persons not falling within the above noted exemptions to the requirement to obtain an employment authorization on the basis of the temporariness of the persons' entry to Canada (i.e., tourists) and common sense.

The definition of tourist or non-student and non-employment related visitor status, is restricted to the exemptions set out below under: (1) student related activities which do not require a student authorization; and (2) employment related activities which do not require an employment authorization.

3.1.1 STUDENT-RELATED ACTIVITIES WHICH DO NOT REQUIRE A STUDENT AUTHORIZATION

- A person seeking entry into Canada for the purposes of attending university or college to take an academic professional or vocational training course is not required to obtain a student authorization prior to engaging in studies if:

  - the person is the dependant of a diplomatic counsellor/officer, representative of official, properly accredited of a country other than Canada or the United Nations or any of its agencies or of any intergovernmental organization of which Canada is a member; and/or

  - the course of studies relates to French and English for a period of three months or less in duration.

- If the course of study does not fall within the definition of a student authorization the individual is exempted from obtaining a student authorization prior to attending the educational institution, school or educational centre.

"Student Authorization" is defined in section 2 of the *Regulations*:

> "student authorization" means a document issued by an immigration officer whereby the person to whom it is issued is authorized
>
> (a) to attend a university or college authorized by statute or charter to confer degrees, or
>
> (b) to take an academic, professional or vocational training course at a university, college or other institution not described in paragraph (a).

- Children attending day care centres or nurseries and individuals taking self-improvement or skills facilitation courses at local school boards or similar institutions are not required to obtain a student authorization.

3.1.2 EMPLOYMENT-RELATED ACTIVITIES WHICH DO NOT REQUIRE AN EMPLOYMENT AUTHORIZATION

Many kinds of employment, or employment related activities, do not require persons entering Canada to apply for an employment authorization. Persons falling within one of the exemptions to the requirement to obtain an employment authorization, may enter Canada as visitors without the additional requirement of applying for an employment authorization.

- Section 19(1) of the *Regulations* sets out the kinds of activities which qualify for visitor status.

  - The activities identified in section 19(1) are employment authorization exempt because the person would require entry into Canada regardless of the labour market and unemployment conditions in Canada at the time.

  - These exemptions relate to continuing activities involving reciprocal international treatment, or religious, political, trade or international business activities, or unique skills which the foreigner will bring temporarily to Canada.

(a) Properly Accredited Diplomats, Consular Officers, Representatives or Officials [19(1)(a)]

. . . a properly accredited diplomat, consular officer, representative or official

(i) of a country, other than Canada,

(ii) of the United Nations or any of its agencies, or

(iii) of any intergovernmental organization in which Canada participates, or

as a member of the suite of any such diplomat, consular officer, representative or official
. . .

- This exemption applies to diplomats as well as their support staff and servants directly involved in relation to the diplomatic activities in Canada, as well as locally engaged staff, unless the sole purpose for the locally engaged em-

59

ployee's entry to Canada is to become locally engaged at a diplomatic, or consular mission.

(b) Military Personnel [19(1)(b)]

... as a member of the armed forces of a country that is a designated state for the purposes of the *Visiting Forces Act*, including a person who has been designated as a civilian component of that visiting force pursuant to paragraph 4(c) of the Act . . .

- This exemption relates to military and civilian component personnel which come within the ambit of the *Visiting Forces Act.*

  Section 15.04(1) of the Act states that immigration officers should not impose terms and conditions of entry on a member of the visiting force or limit her or his period of stay in Canada but that the duration of the member and her or his dependants' stay in Canada should be "for the duration of status".

(c) Clergy and Related Work [19(1)(c)]

... as a clergyman, a member of a religious order or a lay person to assist a congregation or a group in the achievement of its spiritual goals where the duties to be performed by that person will consist mainly of preaching of doctrine, presiding at liturgical functions or spiritual counselling . . .

- This exemption relating to clergy includes members of religious orders as well as lay persons.

- Applicants qualifying for this exemption will be required to be involved in the church or religious group as spiritual counsellors or leaders at a ministerial and non-ministerial level rather than at a practical level (*i.e., support staff, such as bookkeepers, secretaries, music directors, or teachers of mind and body building techniques, etc.*).

- Applicants need not necessarily participate in the religious services of the congregation or group but may provide counselling if it relates to the religious or spiritual goals of the congregation or group.

- The applicants' duties should include preaching to a group and presiding over liturgies for a congregation.

The *Immigration Manual* summarizes this section as follows:

> . . . the person envisaged by R. 19(1)(c) will:- (i) come forward to assist in leading a group or congregation and (ii) perform duties compatible with the attainment of spiritual pursuits by that group or congregation.

(d) Performing Artists [19(1)(d)]

> . . . as a performing artist, a member of a group of performing artists or a member of the staff of the performing artists or the group, where the artist or the group and the staff that accompanies the artist or the group, as the case may be, number not less than 15 . . .

This category is expansive in relation to the entry of performers and related personnel to Canada.

- Incoming performing artists will be required to provide proof of a performance contract in Canada.

- The phrase "members of the staff" relates to persons who are not artists, but whose presence is "integral" to the performance. This would include all staff in possession of skills or knowledge unique to the performance and those who required comprehensive training or specific preparation in relation to their unique "off stage" contributions to the performance.

(e) Crew Members and International Trucking [19(1)(e)]

> . . . as a member of the crew of a vehicle of foreign ownership or foreign registry engaged predominantly in the international transportation of goods or passengers . . .

- This exemption does not apply to the loading and unloading of foreign drivers or the pick up of goods by foreign drivers at one location in Canada for delivery to another location in Canada.

- The exemption applies to drivers who have expertise in the handling of loads of chemicals, furniture, livestock, etc. and who are required to be responsible for loading and unloading of the vehicles because of such expertise.

(f) News Reporting Personnel [19(1)(f)]

. . . as an employee of a foreign news company for the purpose of reporting on Canadian events . . .

- This exemption includes news reporters and their crews and does not include managerial or clerical personnel.

(g) Buyers [19(1)(g)]

. . . as a representative of a business carrying on activities outside Canada or of a foreign government for the purpose of purchasing Canadian goods or services for that business or foreign government, including a person coming to or in Canada for the purpose of

(i) inspecting, during or after manufacturing, the quality of the goods purchased, or

(ii) acquiring training or familiarization with the goods or services purchased,

where that representative will not be actively engaged in production of goods or services in Canada . . .

This section applies to foreign representatives who wish to engage in a plethora of sales related activities. Such activities include the right to enter Canada at any time for the purpose of inspection or training in relation to the goods purchased.

- This section allows the entry into Canada of foreign representatives for the purpose of arranging the export of the goods or to take advantage of services or technology which are somehow related to the goods.

- Foreign representatives may not assist or contribute in the production of goods or services. *Accordingly, any training which may necessarily involve the development of the product or service in any manner whatsoever, is prohibited.*

Given the fact that this section also includes services, the possibilities which are unveiled by this provision for all whom require access to Canada are legion.

(h) Sellers [19(1)(h)]

. . . as a representative of a business carrying on activities outside Canada or of a foreign government coming to or in Canada for a period of less than 90 days for the purpose of selling goods or services for that business or foreign government, where that representative will not be engaged in making sales to the general public . . .

This section has been amended to deal with both goods *and* services.

- Representatives may remain in Canada for a period not exceeding ninety days.

- Applicants may be:

  ° sales representatives of the foreign company selling the goods or services;

  ° persons who enter to arrange for the export of goods to Canada;

  ° individuals meeting with Canadian company personnel to arrange for the delivery of services or distribution of the goods;

  ° and suppliers' representatives making follow-up sales visits not related to the repair or servicing of the equipment *(in which case, they would qualify for an employment authorization under section 20(5)(e) of the Regulations).*

- Representatives are forbidden from making sales to the "general public". The *Immigration Manual, section IS15.04(1)(8), clarifies that the "general public" ". . . is interpreted to mean sales which are for one's own personal consumption. Sales which are authorized under this sec-*

tion include sales to wholesalers, retailers, institutions and businesses which would use the product for their business . . ."

- This section also applies to the entry of business visitors under the GATS *(see Chapter 5).*

(i) Corporation and Union Employees [19(1)(i)]

. . . as a permanent employee of a corporation, union or other organization carrying on business or operating outside Canada who is coming to or in Canada for a period of less than 90 days for the purpose of consulting with other employees or members of that corporation, union or other organization, or inspecting a Canadian branch office or headquarters on behalf of that corporation, union or other organization . . .

- This section applies to the entry to Canada of employees of a company, union, or organization for the purpose of consultation, monitoring, negotiating, auditing and/or inspection within their own company framework.

- Persons who are not actual employees of the company, such as auditors, negotiators, mediators or conciliators who are hired by the company are not included in this section because they are not permanent employees of the corporation, union or other organization.

(j) Emergency Service [19(1)(j)]

. . . for the purpose of rendering emergency, medical or other services for the preservation of life or property . . .

"Emergency" means natural disasters, such as floods, tornadoes, earthquakes, fires, or industrial or commercial accidents threatening the environment.

"Medical" emergencies means situations where admission would facilitate medical procedures relating to a health professional or an organ donor.

- Persons allowed entry to Canada in the case of emergency include doctors or medical teams and appraisers and insurance adjusters.

- Although there are few agreements between Canada and the United States in relation to the entry of persons to Canada in the case of emergency, regardless of such agreements all persons entering Canada for purposes of providing emergency assistance enter Canada under this section.

- If the situation is not an emergency, it comes within the ambit of one of the agreements between Canada and the United States, and persons seeking entry would, nonetheless, require an employment authorization.

(k) Athletes [19(1)(k)]

. . . as a member of a non-Canadian-based team to engage or assist in sport activities or events or as an individual participant to engage in sports activities or events other than as a referee, umpire or similar official . . .

- This exemption applies to foreign teams and individual athletes entering Canada for the purpose of participating in sports activities in Canada.

- In both cases operating personnel are also exempted from the requirement to obtain an employment authorization.

- This exemption also applies to the following groups:

    ° recreational sports activities not involving remuneration;

    ° players and team members who come to Canada for trials;

    ° individual participants competing as individuals in competitions;

    ° racing stable personnel from foreign based stables;

    ° freelance jockeys and race car drivers destined to foreign based stables or clubs, and their agents;

      ○ Olympic or amateur wrestlers who seek entry as part of a non-Canadian based team; and

      ○ individual wrestlers (Olympic or amateur) involved with Canadian organizations.

- Referees, umpires, game officials and professional and semi-professional players must obtain employment authorizations prior to entering Canada.

(l) Judges, Referees [19(1)(l)]

. . . as a judge, referee or similar official in an international sporting event organized by an international amateur sporting association and hosted by a Canadian organization . . .

- Where an international sporting event hosted in Canada is sponsored by a Canadian organization, judges, referees, adjudicators (in the case of music or dance festivals) and other similar officials, may enter Canada under visitor status.

(m) Judges of Animal Show Competitions [19(1)(m)]

. . . as a judge at an animal show competition . . .

- Judges at animal show competitions and agricultural competitions are included under the exemption to the requirement to obtain an employment authorization.

(n) Examiners of Degree-Qualifying Thesis or Project [19(1)(n)]

. . . as an external examiner of a degree-qualifying thesis or project . . .

- This exemption provides the opportunity for Canadian scholars to obtain the instruction, tutelage or supervision by internationally recognized scholars, or foreign scholars possessing eminent qualifications. Foreign scholars, professors and tutors, are, therefore, allowed to enter Canada for the purpose of directing studies, reviewing scholarly performance, examining students, reviewing theses, etc.

- This section also provides foreign professors with the opportunity to enter Canada under visitor status, where their entry relates to the appraisal, examination or evaluation of academic programs, whether they involve course work, instructional materials, computer tutorials, and other similar teaching aids.

- Included in this section is entry by foreign professors to provide consultation on strictly academic matters.

(o) Guest Speakers [19(1)(o)]

. . . as a guest speaker for the sole purpose of making a speech or delivering a paper at a dinner, graduation, convention or similar function . . .

Immigration officers have, due to widespread abuse of this section, adopted a somewhat narrower approach to this exemption than is merited upon a literal reading.

- This section applies to persons who are speaking at conventions, graduations, dinners or similar functions and applies regardless of whether the person is compensated in addition to the payment of expenses and an honorarium in relation to their stay in Canada.

- The section also includes persons who enter Canada for the purposes of giving academic, teaching or research related activities or seminars or workshops, provided that they are not involved in the organizational aspects of the seminars or workshops and have no monetary interest in the seminars or workshops other than the honorarium or fee received.

(p) Expert Witnesses [19(1)(p)]

> . . . as an expert witness for the sole purpose of testifying in proceedings before a
> regulatory board or tribunal or a court . . .

- Expert witnesses are allowed to enter Canada for purposes
  of testifying where such expertise is unique and Canadians
  have not developed this expertise because it is not generally required.

- Persons qualifying under this section will require employment authorizations for any work other than testifying and
  providing information or related analysis or examination.

(q) Personal Servants [19(1)(q)]

> . . . as a permanently employed personal servant coming into or in Canada for a period
> of less than 90 days for the purpose of performing his regular duties with his employer
> during the latter's sojourn in Canada.

- This section applies to personal servants who enter Canada with their employers to continue to provide services
  for a period of less than 90 days.

(r) Officers of Foreign Governments [19(1)(r)]

> . . . as an officer of a foreign government sent by his government to take up duties with
> a federal or provincial agency pursuant to an exchange agreement with Canada . . .

The *Immigration Manual*, Chapter 15.04(3)(r) summarizes this section as follows:

> Canada has concluded agreements with other nations (among which Australia is the
> most visible) which provide for periods of employment in each other's territory at the
> federal or provincial levels. Because other nations do not require Canadian participants
> to have employment authorizations, such foreign participants have also been exempted
> from this requirement.

- This section applies to reciprocal agreements between
  Canada and other nations which would allow a national of

a signatory state the opportunity to work in a government position in Canada (if otherwise accepted) without the requirement to obtain an employment authorization.

(s) Medical Elective or Clinical Clerks [19(1)(s)]

... as a medical elective or clinical clerk at a Canadian medical teaching institution, where that person will merely be observing clinical or medical procedures ...

- This section applies to medical students who are required to undergo clinical training early in their course of study of an observatory nature not involving hands on training.

(t) Trainees with Canadian Parent or Subsidiary Corporation [19(1)(t)]

... as a trainee with a Canadian parent or subsidary corporation, where that trainee will not be actively engaged in the production of goods or services ...

- This exemption is meant to provide multinational corporations with the opportunity to train their foreign employees in a classroom setting in Canada.

- Immigration officers are generally sceptical of any training occurring at a client site or work station, notwithstanding the fact that the trainees are not involved in generating profits for the company (*i.e., production*).

The *Immigration Manual*, Chapter 15.04(3)(t), restricts the training to the classroom and expressly disallows ''hands on'' training, which, according to the *Immigration Manual* requires an employment authorization or validation. The *Immigration Manual* specifies that section 19(1)(t) of the *Regulations* ''. . . parallels that of the United States 'trainee for business' provision and reflects widespread practices in almost every nation.'' Hands-on training at a work site requires an employment authorization given the fact that it is difficult to distinguish between training and actual employment.

(u) Executives and Support Staff Organizing Conventions or Meetings [19(1)(u)]

... as an executive of the organizing committee of a convention or meeting or as a member of the administrative support staff of such a committee who is permanently employed by the organization holding the convention or meeting ...

- Executives and administrative support staff organizing an event are allowed to enter Canada as visitors in the same manner in which delegates attend a convention.

- Persons who are hired specifically for the event and who are not employees of the group who is organizing the event, such as translators, ushers, stenographers or secretaries, are required to obtain employment authorizations.

(v) NAFTA Business Visitors [19(1)(v)]

... as a person pursuant to paragraphs 1 to 3 under the heading "Canada" in Annex 1502.1 of the Agreement as defined in section 2 of the *Canada-United States Free Trade Agreement Implementation Act* is exempted from the requirement to obtain an employment authorization ...

The section referred to in this particular provision relates to the entry of business persons under the Canada-United States of America Free Trade Agreement which was replaced by the North American Free Trade Agreement on January 1, 1994.

- All business visitors who are either United States of America or Mexican citizens, may enter Canada for a period not exceeding six (6) months to engage in the following business visitor activities:

  ○ research and design

  ○ growth

  ○ manufacture and production

  ○ marketing

○ sales

○ distribution

○ after sales service

○ general service

See Chapter 4 for further information about the visitor activities included under the NAFTA.

3.2 APPLYING FOR VISITOR STATUS AT A PORT OF ENTRY—GENERAL REQUIREMENTS

3.2.1 PRESUMPTION OF IMMIGRATION

- Immigration officers will presume that persons seeking to come into Canada seek to live in Canada on a permanent basis.

The general presumption that all visitors seeking entry to Canada are immigrants and that it is the responsibility of the persons seeking entry to satisfy the immigration officers that they are not immigrants is addressed in case law: See *Grewal v. Canada (Min. of Employment and Immigration)* (1989), 8 Imm. L.R. (2d) 100 (Fed. C.A.).

- In cases where a visa is required, a two-step procedure applies in relation to scrutiny of the applicants' purpose for entry to Canada, one at the visa office and one at the port of entry.

3.2.2 BURDEN OF PROOF

Section 8(1) of the *Act* places the burden of proof on persons seeking entry to Canada to demonstrate that they have the right to come into Canada and that their entry would not be contrary to the *Act* or *Regulations*.

3.2.3 APPLYING FOR VISITOR STATUS AT A PORT OF ENTRY

Procedures and documentary requirements relating to visitor status applications at ports of entry vary considerably, depending on the type of visitor status requested.

Obtaining entry to Canada may range from simply advising the customs officer at a port of entry that entry is requested for the purpose of attending an opera (and perhaps having to demonstrate evidence of same by showing the tickets to the customs officer) to undergoing a two hour interview with a senior immigration officer in more complicated situations, such as after-sales situations.

- Individuals applying for entry as tourists or under one of the exemptions to the requirement to obtain a student or employment authorization may apply in one of the following ways:

  ○ processing post abroad;

  ○ port of entry; or

  ○ inland (*in more limited circumstances, set out infra*).

(a) Applying at a Processing Post Abroad

Persons qualifying under one of the exemptions to the requirement to obtain a student or employment authorization will usually not apply at a processing post abroad unless they also require an entry visa because they are not citizens of a proscribed country.

- If an applicant is applying at a processing post abroad, at a minimum, the applicant should provide the type of documentation suggested in Chapter 2 regarding making visitor applications at processing posts abroad.

- The documentation should be specific to the activity under which entry is sought. *For example, if entry is required as an animal show competition judge, proof of credentials and experience as well as the letter of invitation or contract should be provided to immigration officers.*

(b) Port of Entry Applications

- Persons making application for visitor status at a port of entry (who are in possession of an entry visa if required because of their citizenship) may obtain entry to Canada

under any of the exemptions listed in section 19(1) by providing a letter of introduction or a copy of the service agreement as well as a current passport or acceptable travel or
identity document.

• The letter of introduction should be from a Canadian person, company or organization or a foreign person, company or organization as applicable depending on the particular exemption requested.

Examples:

• In the case of exemption 19(1)(g) relating to buyers, the
letter of introduction should generally be provided by the
foreign company and should specify the following:

1. purpose of the foreign worker's entry to Canada;

2. background information in relation to the foreign business;

3. specific information in relation to the Canadian goods
and services purchased;

4. information relating to the Canadian entity from which
those goods and services are to be purchased;

5. the contact person at that entity who may verify the
information contained in the letter of introduction if necessary; and

6. confirmation that the foreign worker will not be actively
engaged in the production of goods or services in Canada.

• If entry is sought under the exemption 19(1)(h) pertaining
to sellers:

○ similar information would appear in the letter of introduction as well as a specification of the actual goods
sold by the business; and

○ A paragraph should be inserted advising immigration officials that the foreign worker is requesting entry for the purpose of selling goods and not services to Canada and that the foreign worker would not be engaged in making sales to the general public.

- In the case of 19(1)(i) pertaining to corporation and union employees:

  ○ the letter of introduction should also be provided by the foreign corporation; and

  ○ the letter should specify that the foreign worker will not engage in any work-related activities during her or his stay in Canada but will enter solely for the purpose of consulting with other employees or members of those corporations or unions or inspecting a Canadian branch office or headquarters on behalf of those unions or corporations.

- Applicants should provide corroborative documentation from a second source for greater certainty of admission.

  For example, in the event that an employee enters Canada for the purpose of inspecting the Canadian branch office, she or he may wish to present documentation from the foreign corporation as well as a letter from the Canadian branch office inviting the foreign worker to come to Canada to inspect the branch office and providing specific information in relation to the branch office as well as information about the inspection duties of the foreign worker.

- Applicants should also demonstrate the following by presenting documentary evidence if possible:

  ○ that the applicant has or will have sufficient funds to support herself or himself while in Canada;

  ○ evidence of return transportation if the visit will be brief; and

○ letter of leave from her or his employer.

(c) Inland Applications

Inland applications are generally made by persons who do not require an entry visa given the fact that they are already in Canada, unless of course, they are seeking an extension of their tourist visa.

- Applicants would be required to complete a form entitled "Application to Change or Extend Status" and would be required to provide the following documents:

  ○ original or copy of passport of applicant;

  ○ documentation demonstrating that entry is requested to perform an activity listed in one of the exemptions to the requirement to obtain an employment or student authorization; and

  ○ a processing fee.

4^1

THE NORTH AMERICAN FREE TRADE AGREEMENT

4.1 INTRODUCTION

The purpose of the North American Free Trade Agreement (''NAFTA'') is to facilitate the movement of goods, services and people amongst its three signatory countries. It establishes that preferential trading arrangement between Canada and the United States has been expanded to include Mexico[2] and is designed to gradually abolish tariffs and trade barriers.

The NAFTA came into force on January 1, 1994. Prior to the existence of the NAFTA, Canada and the United States were parties to the Canada-U.S. Free Trade Agreement (''FTA''). With the implementation of the NAFTA, the FTA was superseded and suspended. However, this suspension is contingent on the continuation of the NAFTA. Should the NAFTA cease to operate, the FTA would be re-instituted between Canada and the United States. The immigration-related provisions of the FTA and the NAFTA are almost identical with the exception of a few substantive and procedural aspects.

The NAFTA does not facilitate immigration or permanent settlement in a signatory country. However, some of the provisions contained in Chapter 16 of the NAFTA allow for virtually indefinite residence in a signatory country provided that an applicant's business or employment opportunity continues without interruption.

Chapter 16 of the NAFTA's priority is to address the temporary entry of persons under four specific categories which will be explored in detail in this chapter: (1) business visitors; (2) professionals; (3) intra-company transferees; and (4) traders and investors. It does not facilitate the entry of individuals who are seeking temporary entry to Canada to replace Canadian workers engaged in a labour dispute.

The NAFTA has been incorporated into Canadian immigration legislation under the general entry provisions which apply to foreign workers. Specifically, the business visitor category was implemented by adding paragraph (w) to section 19(1) of

---

1 Co-authored by Nan Berezowski.
2 Employment & Immigration Canada, *Immigration Manual: Selection & Control* (Ottawa: Canada Communications Group-Publishing Supply and Services Canada, 1994), c. 16, p. 1.

the *Immigration Regulations* (*Regulations*). All other categories fall within the ambit of section 20(5)(b)(i) of the *Regulations*, as amended, to include bilateral and multilateral agreements.

4.2 BUSINESS VISITORS

4.2.1

(a) Definition of Business Visitors

"Business visitors" are business persons who plan to carry on business activity related to research and design, growth, manufacturing and production, marketing, sales and distribution, after-sales service and general sales.

(b) Business Activities

- The business activities contemplated are set out in Chapter 16 of the NAFTA. They are commercial in nature and involve aspects of business in the following seven defined areas:

  ○ Research and Design

  ○ Growth, Manufacture and Production

  ○ Marketing

  ○ Sales

  ○ Distribution

  ○ After-Sales Service

  ○ General Service

- Attached as Appendix 4-A is a reproduction of Appendix 1603.A.1 of the NAFTA which lists the specific activities which qualify under the general categories of business activities listed above.

○ Appendix 4-A contains some provisions which at first instance appear to be inconsistent with the business visitor criteria and, as such, warrant close review. Some activities, although not strictly business related, are nonetheless permissible. *For instance, a harvester owner supervising a harvesting crew is contemplated under the Growth, Manufacture and Production category.*

(c) Managers and Financial Service Personnel

- This category includes:

  ○ Management and supervisory personnel engaging in a commercial transaction for an enterprise in the United States or Mexico.

  ○ Financial services personnel who enter Canada for a commercial transaction for a company located in the United States or Mexico *(i.e., insurers, bankers or financial/investment brokers).*

  ○ Public relations personnel who enter Canada to consult with clients, business associates, colleagues or customers or to participate in a convention.

4.2.2 QUALIFICATIONS AND REQUIREMENTS

(a) General Requirements

- In order to qualify as a business visitor applicants are required to satisfy the following general requirements:

  ○ They must hold a United States or Mexican citizenship.

  ○ Their activities in Canada must fall within the ambit of the visitor activities listed in Appendix 1603.A.1 of Chapter 16 of the NAFTA, attached hereto as Appendix 4-A. *Typical business activities include, but are not limited to,*

consultation, negotiation, discussion, research, partici-
pation in educational, professional or business conven-
tions or meetings and soliciting business.

○ They should remain an employee of the foreign enterprise or, if self-employed, their place of business must
remain outside of Canada, and they must intend to enter
Canada temporarily in a non-employment capacity.

○ Their main source of remuneration must be from a
source outside of Canada, although payment of expenses incidental to business travel, and honorariums
will not generally bar the applicants. *Immigration officials*
are instructed to consider those who are paid in Canada
as employed in Canada and accordingly, will not permit
them to qualify as business visitors.

○ The foreign enterprise's profits must accumulate primarily outside of Canada.

○ Although often difficult to determine, business visitors
must also demonstrate that the activities performed are
international in scope. In short, that their business interests must relate to one of the other NAFTA signatories
apart from Canada.

(b) After-Sales Services

• After-sales services include the installation, repair or periodic servicing of commercial or industrial equipment or
machinery or computer software. They do not include operating the equipment, machinery or computer software for
production.

• The essential component of after-sales service is that it
must involve specialized knowledge essential to the seller's
contractual obligations. *The service must be something*
which cannot be easily performed and must involve some
expertise.

- Persons applying pursuant to the after-sales services provisions must satisfy the following additional requirements:

  ○ They must possess the level of skill or knowledge necessary to perform the function.

  ○ The level of skill must be evidenced by post secondary education relevant to the area of service or by licensing, certification or accreditation issued by an authoritative body.

  ○ They must possess additional in-class or on-site training which is essential to providing the service.

  ○ They must be employed by a United States or Mexican company.

  ○ The equipment or machinery (including computer software) must be for commercial or industrial use.

  ○ The equipment or machinery must be manufactured and purchased outside of Canada.

  ○ The services must be performed pursuant to an original sales contract which involves a warranty or service contract.

  ○ The service must be performed during the life of the warranty or service contract or extension.

  ○ The services to be rendered must be set out in the service or warranty agreement or sales contract or extension.

There are a few special requirements applicable to the after-sales services provided in relation to computer software. Specifically, the term "purchase of computer software" includes licensing agreements. Furthermore, entry to Canada will be allowed for the purpose of performing after-sales services on computer software where the purchase by the Canadian company is made with a Canadian affiliate or Canadian distributor of a foreign manufacturer. The assumption in forming this exemption is that, the Canadian affiliate or distributor may not be equipped to provide installation services, repair services or the periodic servicing and testing required.

In the case of leases, there must be some clear nexus between the Canadian purchaser and the United States or Mexican seller. Accordingly, the initial transaction must relate to a sale.

(c) Professions Pursuant to the General Services Category

As stated above, Appendix 4-A lists a number of activities which qualify as "General Service" functions. This subcategory applies to professionals who engage in business activities at a professional level.

- Professionals are described in Appendix 1603.D.1, attached hereto as Appendix 4-B.

    o Applicants must be seeking entry to Canada for business purposes, but cannot anticipate entering the labour market.

    o They must not receive remuneration in Canada.

    o They must satisfy the specific qualification requirements set out in Appendix 1603.D.1.

4.2.3 DOCUMENTATION REQUIRED IN SUPPORT OF APPLICATION

- Business persons seeking entry into Canada may be required to provide documentation which proves that their activity falls within the ambit of one or more of the subcategories applicable to business visitors.

    As the NAFTA provisions were intended to be facilitative in nature, immigration officials are instructed to give applicants every opportunity to establish that they have satisfed the business visitor admission criteria. Accordingly, an applicant's verbal statement that her or his business is being carried on outside of Canada or an alternative *indication of same, such as her or his business card or enterprises advertisements, may suffice. However, in most instances, where possible the applicant should provide a letter from the employer confirming the details of the business. Such documentation will facilitate the job of the immigration officer.*

- Applicants should provide a letter from the United States or Mexican employer confirming the particulars of their duties and specifying the subcategory under which the application would fall *(i.e., research and design, growth, manufacture and production, marketing, sales, distribution, after-sales service and general service).*

- The letter should also state the following:

  ○ the primary source of remuneration is outside of Canada;

  ○ the applicant's main source of business is outside of Canada and the profits of the company are accumulated outside of Canada;

  ○ the applicant continues to be employed outside of Canada and will be returning to her or his employment outside of Canada after the temporary entry to Canada;

  ○ the applicant's entry to Canada is related to her or his employment in the United States or Mexico; and

  ○ the applicant's intended business activities in Canada.

- Applicants falling within the ambit of the business visitor subcategory relating to after-sales service are also required to provide copies of the original sales, warranty or service agreement and extensions of such agreements. If copies are not available at the time of entry, the employer may send a copy by facsimile transmission to the immigration officer.

4.2.4 THE APPLICATION PROCESS

(a) Where to Apply

- Business visitors must apply at the port of entry in the same manner as persons covered by section 19(1) of the *Regulations*. An application cannot be made prior to arriving in Canada.

- Business visitors can be admitted at the Primary Inspection Line, except those applying for entry under the after-sales service provision of Appendix 1603.A.1 who must be referred to Canada Immigration for secondary examination.

(b) Documents Issued

- Generally, when entry is sought under the business visitor category, no documentation is provided to the applicant at the port of entry. However in the case of entry under the after-sales service or general service business activities, however, immigration officers are required to provide visitor records to any business persons entering Canada for a period of more than two days to perform installation or dismantling work or to provide servicing, training or supervision.

- Business visitors will often seek entry to Canada for a number of regular visits taking place over a period of weeks or months. In such circumstances:

  ○ establish the purpose of entry, and

  ○ obtain a visitor record on their behalf so as to facilitate their entry and reduce the number of potential referrals to immigration secondary.

(c) Duration

Visitr status, as addressed in Chapter 2, is provided for up to a period of six months. However, in cases where a visitor record is not required or provided, visitors to

Canada are nonetheless authorized to enter and remain in Canada for a period of up to six months. However, it is generally assumed that business persons seeking entry as visitors under the NAFTA will remain in Canada for a brief period of time for the purpose of accomplishing their task.

- Successful applicants will be coded "FTA" or "054".

4.3 PROFESSIONALS

The provisions of the NAFTA relating to professionals represent the most significant expansion of Canada's policy toward temporary foreign workers in recent years. The provisions expand upon those who could qualify for employment authorizations and simplify entry.

- Like the intra-company transferee and treaty trader/investor provisions of the NAFTA, professionals may obtain employment authorizations without having to first obtain job validation from the Canada Employment Centre.

4.3.1 QUALIFICATIONS AND REQUIREMENTS

- To obtain an employment authorization pursuant to the NAFTA, the applicant must meet the following requirements:

  ◦ The applicant must be a citizen of either the United States or Mexico.

  ◦ The applicant must be coming to Canada to practise a profession identified in Appendix 1603.D.1 of the NAFTA.

  ◦ The applicant must be qualified to work in the profession for which entry is sought.

  Appendix 1603.D.1 sets out the minimum educational and or work related experience, for each particular profession listed. These requirements represent the minimum criteria for entry and do not necessarily reflect the educational, accreditation or licensing requirements necessary to prac-

tise a profession in Canada. In other words, the immigration authorities will not require that applicants be licensed in their professions, even if those professions are licensable in the jurisdiction to which that individual seeks entry. Appendix 1603.D.1 itself does not impose this requirement.

When the minimum requirement for a profession is a baccalaureate degree, then the degree need not be in the exact field of the profession; it could be in a closely related field. For example, a computer software programmer with a degree in engineering could qualify.

Applicants who are required to have baccalaureate or licenciatura degrees are not required to have obtained these degrees in Canada, the United States of America or Mexico. By contrast, post-secondary diplomas which would qualify an applicant for entry must be from an institution in either Canada, the United States or Mexico.

- The applicant must be entering Canada to engage in pre-arranged employment with a Canadian employer.

The professional provisions of the NAFTA do not apply to self-employed individuals, meaning individuals who are coming to Canada to work for themselves to provide services in their profession to a number of Canadian clients or customers. This exclusion encompasses situations where the Canadian enterprise is owned or substantially controlled by the applicant. It is important to note, however, that a professional can work in Canada on more than one contract at a time. In such a case, information on each Canadian enterprise must appear in the employer field of the employment authorization(s).

- The applicant must be coming to Canada to provide professional level services in the field of qualification.

The typical example is that an accountant cannot enter as a NAFTA professional to perform services as a bookkeeper. However, the converse is acceptable: for exam-

ple, an engineer may enter Canada as a professional to be an executive in an enterprise, such as vice-president. However in the performance of the duties of vice-president, the engineer would have to bring to bear engineering knowledge which would be required to perform the position of vice-president.

- The applicant must comply with existing immigration requirements for temporary entry.

The business visitor provisions of the NAFTA, under the General Service provision of Appendix 1603.A.1, provide that professionals seeking entry into Canada for less than ninety days may be admitted as business visitors without obtaining employment authorizations or paying the required cost recovery fee. These persons would not be seeking to enter the labour market rather; they would be seeking to perform activities such as soliciting business, consulting, providing advice and meeting clients.

4.3.2 DOCUMENTATION REQUIRED IN SUPPORT OF APPLICATION

- The following documents are required to support an application:

  ○ Photocopy of the applicant's United States or Mexican birth certificate, citizenship certificate or passport.

  ○ A letter from the Canadian enterprise to which the applicant is destined, or from the applicant's United States or Mexican employer on whose behalf the applicant will render services to a Canadian enterprise, stating the following:

    1. the identity of the proposed employer in Canada;

    2. the profession which the applicant will exercise in Canada;

    3. the applicant's job title;

4. the applicant's job description;

5. the arrangements for the applicant's remuneration while the applicant is in Canada, including source and amount;

6. the applicant's qualifications for entry under the NAFTA as well as for the position itself; and

7. confirmation that the position is temporary in nature and that an employment authorization is being sought for a period of one year.

○ Evidence of the applicant's related experience (included in employer's letter, or reference letter from a previous employer).

○ Evidence that the applicant meets the qualifications stated in Appendix 1603.D.1 in the form of photocopies of degrees, diplomas, professional licenses, accreditation or registration, etc.

○ The required application fee.

4.3.3 THE APPLICATION PROCESS

(a) Where to Apply

• A NAFTA professional application may be submitted to Canadian visa offices abroad, to a Canada immigration office at a port of entry, or to the Case Processing Centre in Vegreville, Alberta if the applicant is already in Canada as a business visitor.

(b) Duration and Extensions

• Employment authorizations issued to professionals have a maximum duration of one year but they are renewable annually for so long as the NAFTA is in force. *Note, however, that the longer a person remains in Canada as a NAFTA professional, the more questions will be asked about whether that individual has developed a permanent intent to reside in Canada rather than mere temporary intent.*

- If the NAFTA professional has formed a permanent intent to reside in Canada she or he should be counselled to obtain Canadian permanent resident status.

4.4 INTRA-COMPANY TRANSFEREES

4.4.1 DEFINITION OF INTRA-COMPANY TRANSFEREES

"Intra-company transferees" are business persons employed by an enterprise seeking to render services to a branch, parent, subsidiary or affiliate of that enterprise, in a managerial or executive capacity or in a manner that involves specialized knowledge.

4.4.2 TERMS

"Branch" means an operating division or office of the same business enterprise housed in a different location.

A "parent" is a firm, corporation or other legal entity that has subsidiaries.

A "subsidiary" is a firm, corporation or other legal entity with a parent that owns, directly or indirectly, half or more than half of the entity and controls the entity; or that owns, directly or indirectly, 50 per cent of a 50/50 joint venture and has equal control and veto power over the entity; or that owns, directly or indirectly, less than half of the entity but in fact controls the entity.

An "affiliate" is one of two subsidiaries, both of which are owned and controlled by the same parent or individual; or one of two legal entities, owned and controlled by the same group of individuals, each individual owning and controlling approximately the same share or proportion of each enterprise.

- Ensure that the business enterprise is actively doing business in both countries.

4.4.3 QUALIFICATIONS AND REQUIREMENTS

- Applicants must have been employed continuously in a senior executive or managerial capacity or one involving "specialized knowledge" for one year in the previous three-year period.

(a) Executive Capacity

- Executive capacity refers to a position in which the employee has the following responsibilities:

  ○ Directs the management of the organization or a major component or function of the organization that establishes the goals and policies of the organization, component, or function.

  ○ Exercises a wide latitude in discretionary decision making.

  ○ Receives only general supervision or direction from higher level executives, the board of directors, or stockholders of the business enterprise.

  The executive does not generally perform duties necessary in the production of a product or in the delivery of a service.

  In smaller businesses, the title of the position might not be sufficient to establish that the position is managerial or executive. For example, an architect who incorporates a business and hires a secretary and a draftsperson will not automatically be considered as holding an executive or managerial position. In order to qualify as a manager or executive as described in the intra-company transferee category, the architect must be engaged in managerial or executive duties rather than pure architectural duties.

90

(b) Managerial Capacity

- Managerial capacity refers to a position in which the employee primarily:

  ◦ Manages the organization, or a department, subdivision function or component of the organization.

  ◦ Supervises and controls the work of other supervisory, professional or managerial employees, or manages an essential function within the organization, or a department or subdivision of the business enterprise.

  ◦ Has the authority to hire and fire and/or recommend other personnel actions such as the granting of promotions and authorization of leave.

  ◦ If no other employee is directly supervised, functions at a senior level within the organization's hierarchy or with respect to the function managed.

  ◦ Exercises discretion over the day-to-day operations of the activity or function over which the employee has the authority.

  The first line supervisor is not considered as acting in a managerial capacity unless the employees supervised are professionals. Like the executive, the manager does not primarily perform tasks required in production of a product or in a delivery of a service. Similarly, in smaller businesses, the title of the position may not be sufficient to establish that a position is managerial or executive.

(c) Specialized Knowledge

- Specialized knowledge refers to knowledge possessed by an individual about the Canadian enterprise's:

  ◦ product

- ○ service

- ○ research

- ○ equipment

- ○ technique

- ○ management

- ○ other interests and applications in international markets

- Specialized knowledge may also refer to an *advanced* level of knowledge or expertise in the organization's processes and procedures.

- A person who possesses an advanced level of knowledge or expertise will usually be in a position critical to the well-being of the enterprise.

In determining whether the applicant possesses specialized knowledge, the immigration official will consider if such knowledge is available in Canada and if it is related to common practices or products. However, neither evidence of unsuccessful recruitment efforts nor job validation will be required in order to demonstrate that such knowledge is not available in Canada.

4.4.4 DOCUMENTATION REQUIRED IN SUPPORT OF APPLICATION

- The following documents are required in support of an application made under this category:

- ○ Proof of United States or Mexican citizenship.

- ○ Confirmation that the applicant has been employed continuously by the United States or Mexican business enterprise for one year within the three-year period immediately preceding the date of the application.

° A letter outlining the applicant's current position in an executive or managerial capacity, or one involving specialized knowledge. *(This letter should include the applicant's position, title, job description, and place in the business enterprise.)*

° If the applicant is applying pursuant to the specialized knowledge category, evidence that the person has such knowledge and that the position in Canada requires such knowledge.

° An outline of the position in Canada. (This refers to the applicants anticipated job description, and place in the business enterprise in Canada.).

° Indication of intended duration of stay in Canada.

° Description of the relationship between the enterprise in Canada and the enterprise in the United States or Mexico.

° Confirmation that the Canadian employer is "doing business" in Canada. "Doing business" is the regular and systematic provision of goods and/or services on a continuing basis by a parent, branch or subsidiary or affiliate; it does not contemplate the mere presence of an agent or office.

° The applicant's current salary and the salary contemplated for the position in Canada.

• Visa officers may also request tangible proof to establish the relationship between the Canadian and the American or Mexican organization.

• An applicant seeking entry to open a new office on behalf of the American or Mexican enterprise may also qualify as an intra-company transferee if it is established that the enterprise in Canada is expected to support a managerial or executive position or, in the case of specialized knowledge, is expected to be doing business.

○ When preparing this portion of the submission, the following factors should be considered:

1. the ownership or control of the enterprise;

2. the premise of the enterprise;

3. the investment committed;

4. the organizational structure;

5. the goods and services to be provided; and

6. the viability of the American or Mexican operation.

4.4.5 THE APPLICATION PROCESS

(a) Where to Apply

• NAFTA intra-company transferee applications may be submitted to:

○ a Canadian visa office abroad;

○ a Canada immigration office at a port of entry; or

○ the Case Processing Centre in Vegreville, Alberta, if the applicant is already in Canada as a business visitor.

(b) Documents Issued

• Those applicants who qualify will be issued an employment authorization. The employment authorization code is VECB24.

• When assessing an applicant as an intra-company transferee under the NAFTA, the general provision for intra-company transferees set out in Regulation 20(5)(e)(i) should be considered. As with respect to executives and managers, the criteria is less restrictive. It does not, however, include the specialized knowledge category.

(c) Duration and Extensions

An employment authorization issued at the time of entry would normally have a maximum duration of one year.

Extensions can be granted for durations of up to two years at a time, assuming that the individual continues to comply with the requirements for intra-company transferee. However, the intra-company transferee category is the only NAFTA category to have a cap placed on the total duration of employment. The total period of stay for a person employed in an executive or managerial capacity may not exceed seven years. The total period of stay for a person employed in a position requiring specialized knowledge may not exceed five years.

> • Accordingly, the corresponding provisions set out in the regulatory exemptions (see Chapter 6) and the GATS (see Chapter 5) should first be considered, as they are likely to be more beneficial to executives and managers.

4.5 TRADERS

Treaty traders and treaty investors are considered in a combined category under the NAFTA. This category corresponds to the "E" non-immigrant visas of the United States.

4.5.1 DEFINITION OF TRADER

The "trader" is a business person who is seeking temporary entry to carry on substantial trade in goods or services principally between Canada and the United States or Mexico.

4.5.2 TERMS

"Trade" is the exchange, purchase or sale of goods and/or services.

"Goods" are tangible commodities or merchandise having intrinsic value. Money, securities, and negotiable instruments are not considered goods.

''Services'' are economic activities with outputs other than tangible goods. These activities include, but are not confined to, international banking, insurance, transportation, communications and data processing, advertising, accounting, design and engineering, management consulting and tourism.

''Substantial trade'' is determined by both the volume of the trade conducted and the monetary value of the transactions.

- Proof of numerous small transactions, might establish the requisite "continuing course" of international trade.

- The test is whether the person's predominant activity in Canada is international trading.

- In excess of 50 per cent of the total volume of trade conducted in Canada by the enterprise's Canadian office must be between Canada and the United States or Mexico.

4.5.3 QUALIFICATIONS AND REQUIREMENTS

(a) The Applicant

- The applicant must be trading on her or his own behalf, or as an agent of a person or organization engaged in trade principally between Canada and the United States or Mexico. Alternatively, the applicant may also be an employee of a person or corporation maintaining trader status in Canada.

(b) The Enterprise

- The Canadian enterprise must have American or Mexican nationality. That is, the individual or corporate entity that owns at least 50 per cent interest (directly or by stock) in the enterprise established in Canada must hold American or Mexican citizenship.

- Joint ventures and partnerships are limited to two parties.

Determination of parent-subsidiary relationships is governed by the nationality of the corporate entity established in Canada. The jurisdiction of incorporation of an enterprise does not indicate its nationality. Rather, nationality is indicated by ownership.

(c) The Employer (Where Applicable)

- To bring an employee into Canada pursuant to the NAFTA trader provisions, the prospective employer in Canada must satisfy the "nationality" requirement.

  - If the employer is an individual, she or he must be a citizen of the United States or Mexico who is maintaining trader status in Canada.

  - If the prospective employer is a corporation or other business enterprise, as is generally the case, the majority ownership must be held by citizens of the United States or Mexico, who, if not residing in the United States or Mexico, are maintaining trader status in Canada.

- A citizen of the United States or Mexico who is a permanent resident of Canada does *not* qualify to bring an employee into Canada under the trader provisions.

- Similarly, shares of the corporation or other business enterprise owned by a citizen of the United States or Mexico who is a permanent resident of Canada will not be counted in determining majority ownership to qualify the company for bringing in an employee as a trader.

(d) The Employee's Position

The applicant must be employed in a capacity that is supervisory, or executive, or involves essential skills. With respect to the first and second criteria, the supervisory or executive element of the position must be a principal function.

- A supervisor is a manager primarily responsible for directing, controlling and guiding subordinate employees. She or he will not routinely engage in hands-on activities.

A first line supervisor generally will not satisfy these requirements.

- An executive has significant policy authority and is in a primary position in the enterprise.

- Essential skills or services are special qualifications that are vital to the effectiveness of the enterprise's Canadian operations.

The essential employee is not required to be previously employed by the American or Mexican enterprise.

- The visa office abroad will base its evaluation of an employee applying for trader status on the following criteria:

  ° the degree of proven expertise of the applicant in the area of specialization;

  ° the degree to which the special skills are unique;

  ° the function of the job;

  ° the period of the training required to perform the anticipated duties; and

  ° the salary that the special expertise can command.

Individuals who are employed by the enterprise to train or supervise personnel employed in manufacturing, maintenance and repair functions may be granted trader status even though manual duties are performed, provided that the enterprise cannot obtain the service of a comparable qualified Canadian technician. It is expected that the enterprise in Canada will eventually locate and train a Canadian to serve in this capacity. If the training by foreign workers is not accomplished within a reasonable period of time, the failure of the training program will be a basis upon which to refuse repeated requests that an American or Mexican enter Canada for the purpose of training and supervising.

4.5.4 DOCUMENTATION REQUIRED IN SUPPORT OF APPLICATION

- Completed and Signed Application for Temporary Entry to Canada (Employment Authorization) (IMM 1295).

- Completed and Signed Trader/Investor Status (IMM 5321) Application form (attached hereto as Appendix 4-C).

- Proof of the applicant's United States or Mexican citizenship in the form of a copy of her or his passport or Certificate of Birth.

- Letter attesting to ownership of the corporation from its secretary or in-house counsel.

- The requisite non-refundable employment authorization processing fee in the amount of CDN$125.00.

4.5.5 THE APPLICATION PROCESS

(a) Application Form

- Persons applying for trader status must complete both the Application for Temporary Entry to Canada (IMM 1295) and the Trader/Investor Status (IMM 5321) form. The latter may be provided by any Canadian embassy, consulate or immigration office.

(b) Where to Apply

- For reasons of client service, program consistency and reciprocity, an application by a United States or Mexican citizen for an employment authorization made pursuant to the trader provisions must normally be submitted to a visa office abroad. However, pursuant to section 19(4)(p) of the *Regulations*, Mexican citizens who have been granted visitor status can also apply for trader status from within Canada.

(c) Documents Issued

- Qualified persons will be issued an employment authorization with the validation exempt code VEC-21.

(d) Duration and Extensions

The initial employment authorization can have a maximum duration of one year. Immigration officials have the discretion to grant extensions for a duration of two years provided that the applicant continues to meet the aforementioned criteria.

- Applications to extend can be made from within Canada by submitting the Application to Change Terms and Conditions or Extend My Stay in Canada (IMM 1249). Alternatively, a new application, specifically stating the circumstances of the applicant's present status in Canada can be made to a visa office abroad.

Visa officers are instructed to compare the contents of the documentation in support of the original application with the documentation provided in support of the request for an extension. Moreover, in the case of prolonged and/or indefinite stays in Canada under this status, an officer may express concern about the issue of "temporary intent". The applicants' expression of a definite intent to return to the United States or Mexico upon termination of trader status will generally be accepted as sufficient evidence about the temporariness of their stay in Canada, unless there are indications to the contrary.

- Trader status terminates if the applicant assumes another position of employment in an activity inconsistent with this status, upon dissolution of the company or on termination of the business activity.

4.6 INVESTORS

4.6.1 DEFINITION OF INVESTOR

"Investors" are business persons who seek temporary entry to develop and direct the operations of an enterprise in which they have invested, or are actively in the process of investing, a substantial amount of capital.

4.6.2 QUALIFICATIONS AND REQUIREMENTS

(a) Develop and Direct

- To satisfy the "develop and direct" requirement the applicant should have a controlling interest in the enterprise.

º An interest of 50 per cent or less will generally not satisfy the control requirement. *Where there has been United States or Mexican corporate investment in Canadian-based corporations, immigration officers have been instructed to focus on corporate practice as opposed to an arithmetic formula, as control of half or less of the stock may nevertheless result in effective control of the corporation.*

º An equal share of the investment, such as an equal partnership, will not generally be considered a controlling investment in a Canadian-based corporation.

º A joint venture may meet the "develop and direct" requirement, provided that the United States or Mexican corporation can demonstrate that it has, in effect, operational control of the enterprise.

(b) The Investment

Immigration officials will assess the nature of the transaction to determine whether a particular financial arrangement qualifies as an investment.

• The investment requirement contemplates the placing of funds or other capital assets at risk in order to generate a profit or return. If funds are not subject to partial or total loss, the investment requirement is not met.

• Before making a submission that the applicant's particular financial arrangement qualifies as an investment, the reasonable total investment amount needed to establish the business must be determined.

• Only the amount already invested or irrevocably committed to the investment can be considered in determining the substantiality of the investment. *Prospective investment arrangements and mere intent to invest are insufficient. There must be a present commitment. The applicant must be approaching the commencement of business opera-*

tions. This entails a commitment beyond the contract sign-
ing, location scouting, and even property purchasing stage.

The investment will be evaluated in light of the total financial commitment to the enterprise. This total investment is the cost of an established business, or the money needed to establish the business. For example, the total amount required to establish a consulting service will likely be considerably less than that required to commence a manufacturing plant or restaurant. Consequently, an amount deemed sufficient for one enterprise may not be considered sufficient for another.

In businesses where the total investment is relatively small, the investor will be expected to contribute a proportionately large amount; where the total investment has been large, the percentage of investment required will be comparatively less.

- An applicant is not entitled to this status if the investment, even if substantial, is unlikely to return more than enough income to support the applicant and her or his family. *This is because the objective of the investor status is to promote investment in Canada.*

- Investor status cannot be extended to non-profit organi-zations.

- The applicant must demonstrate prior or present posses-sion and control of the funds or capital assets. "Funds" may consist of a reasonable amount of cash held in a business bank account or similar vessel used to facilitate routine business operations. *Mere possession of uncom-mitted funds in a bank account will be unlikely to qualify.*

- Indebtedness such as a mortgage or commercial loan se-cured by the enterprise's assets cannot count toward the investment as it lacks the requisite risk.

  ○ However, consistent with this rationale, where applicants have used their own assets to secure a loan, such as a second mortgage, or have given their personal signa-ture, these assets may be considered.

- Payment in the form of leases or rents for property or equip-ment may be calculated toward the investment in an amount limited to the funds devoted to that item in any one month.

- ○ The market value of leased equipment is not representative of the investment and neither is the annual rental cost unless it has been paid in advance as these rents are generally paid from the current earnings of the business.

- The amount spent for the purchase of equipment and in acquiring inventory may be calculated in the investment total. *The value of these goods or equipment transferred to Canada (for example, factory machinery shipped to Canada to start or expand a plant) will be considered an investment provided that the applicant can demonstrate that the goods or machinery will be put, or are being put, to use in the ongoing commercial enterprise as an investment.*

(c) A Real and Active Enterprise

- The enterprise must be a real and active commercial or entrepreneurial undertaking which operates to produce some service or commodity for profit.

  - ○ It must have a genuine existence. *Mere paper existence will not suffice.*

  - ○ It must be more than a speculative investment. *For instance, a passive investment in developed or undeveloped real estate or stock will not qualify.*

  A plan for future investment, expansion, and/or development will be treated as a significant asset in meeting the aforementioned criterion. Moreover, evidence that the applicant intends and is able to make an additional investment in the future of the enterprise may demonstrate that the business is, or will be, a commercial enterprise in the future.

4.6.3 THE EMPLOYER WHERE THE INVESTOR APPLICANT IS AN EMPLOYEE

Where the investor applicant is an employee, the nationality of the employing business enterprise in Canada is scrutinized.

- The prospective employer must be a citizen of the United States or Canada.

- If the employer is a business enterprise, citizens of the United States or Mexico who, if not residing in the United States or Mexico, are maintaining investor status in Canada, must hold majority ownership.

- A United States or Mexican citizen who is a permanent resident of Canada will not qualify to bring an employee into Canada under this category.

- Similarly, shares of a business enterprise owned by a citizen of the United States or Mexico who is a permanent resident in Canada will not be considered in determining majority ownership to qualify the company for bringing in an employee as an Investor.

- In parent/subsidiary situations it is the nationality of the entity established in Canada that is at issue. Counsel for the applicant should demonstrate nationality through corporate documentation or a solicitor's letter.

4.6.4 DOCUMENTATION REQUIRED IN SUPPORT OF APPLICATION

- Completed and signed Temporary Entry to Canada (Employment Authorization) (IMM1295) Application form.

- Completed and signed Trader/Investor (IMM 5321) Application form.

- Proof of United States or Mexican citizenship.

- Proof that the enterprise to which the applicant is coming has United States or Mexican nationality.

- Evidence that the applicant intends and is able to invest in the enterprise in the future.

- Letters from Chambers of Commerce or statistics from trade associations evidencing that the intended amount of investment is reasonable.

- If the productive nature of the investment is at issue, evidence indicating that the enterprise will expand local employment possibilities and proof that the applicant's primary function will not be that of a skilled or unskilled labourer.

- Evidence of the enterprise's total value such as the purchase price or tax valuation.

- The requisite processing fee.

An established Mexican or United States corporation will be able to demonstrate a substantial investment in Canada by showing its proven record of success in the other treaty country. Given that the credibility of the company has been established and recognised, immigration officers will likely be amenable to waiving some of the above-noted supporting documents on the basis of common sense.

4.6.5 THE APPLICATION PROCESS

(a) Application Forms

- Applicants are required to submit both the Temporary Entry to Canada (Employment Authorization) (IMM1295) and the Traders/Investor (IMM 5321) application forms.

(b) Where to Apply

- An application by an American or Mexican citizen for an employment authorization made pursuant to the investor provisions must normally be submitted to a visa office abroad.

- However, pursuant to section 19(4)(p) of the *Regulations*, Mexican citizens who are granted visitor status can also apply for investor status from within Canada.

(c) Duration and Extension

Visa officers are instructed to compare the contents of the documentation in support of the original application with that provided in support of the request for an extension. Moreover, their attention may be turned to the question of "temporary intent".

Appendix 4-A

Research and Design

- Technical, scientific and statistical researchers conducting independent research, or research for an enterprise located in the territory of another Party.

Growth, Manufacture and Production

- Harvester owner supervising a harvesting crew admitted under applicable law.
- Purchasing and production management personnel conducting commercial transactions for an enterprise located in the territory of another Party.

Marketing

- Market researchers and analysts conducting independent research or analysis, or research or analysis for an enterprise located in the territory of another Party.
- Trade fair and promotional personnel attending a trade convention.

Sales

- Sales representatives and agents taking orders or negotiating contracts for goods or services for an enterprise located in the territory of another Party but not delivering goods or providing services.
- Buyers purchasing for an enterprise located in the territory of another Party.

Distribution

- Transportation operators transporting goods or passengers to the territory of a Party from the territory of another Party or loading and transporting goods or passengers from the territory of a Party to the territory of another Party, with no loading and delivery within the territory of the Party into which entry is sought of goods located in or passengers boarding in that territory.
- With respect to temporary entry into the territory of the United States, Canadian customs brokers performing brokerage duties relating to the export of goods from the territory of the United States to or through the territory of Canada; with respect to temporary entry into the territory of Canada, United States customs brokers performing brokerage duties relating to the export of goods from the territory of Canada to or through the territory of the United States.
- Customs brokers consulting regarding the facilitation of the import or export of goods.

After-Sales Service

- Installers, repair and maintenance personnel and supervisors, possessing specialized knowledge essential to a seller's contractual obligation, performing services or training workers to perform such services, pursuant to a warranty or other service contract incidental to the sale of commercial or industrial equipment or machinery, including computer software, purchased from an enterprise located outside the territory of the Party into which temporary entry is sought, during the life of the warranty or service agreement.

General Service

- Professionals engaging in a business activity at a professional level in a profession set out in Schedule II.

- Management and supervisory personnel engaging in a commercial transaction for an enterprise located in the territory of another Party.

- Financial services personnel (insurers, bankers or investment brokers) engaging in commercial transactions for an enterprise located in the territory of another Party.

- Public relations and advertising personnel consulting with business associates, and attending or participating in conventions.

- Tourism personnel (tour and travel agents, tour guides or tour operators) attending or participating in conventions or conducting a tour that has begun in the territory of another Party.

- Tour bus operators entering the territory of a Party:

    (a) with a group of passengers on a bus tour that has begun in, and will return to, the territory of another Party;

    (b) to meet a group of passengers on a bus tour that will end, and the predominant portion of which will take place, in the territory of another Party; or

    (c) with a group of passengers on a bus tour to be unloaded in the territory of the Party into which temporary entry is sought, and returning with no passengers or reloading with such group for transportation to the territory of another Party.

- Translators or interpreters performing services as employees of an enterprise located in the territory of another Party.

Definitions

For purposes of this Schedule:

"territory of another Party" means the territory of a Party other than the territory of the Party into which temporary entry is sought;

"tour bus operator" means a natural person, including relief personnel accompanying or following to join, necessary for the operation of a tour bus for the duration of a trip; and

"transportation operator" means a natural person, other than a tour bus operator, including relief personnel accompanying or following to join, necessary for the operation of a vehicle for the duration of a trip.

Appendix 4-B

Appendix 1603.D.1
Professionals

PROFESSION[1]	MINIMUM EDUCATION REQUIREMENTS AND ALTERNATIVE CREDENTIALS
General	
Accountant	Baccalaureate or Licenciatura Degree; or C.P.A., C.A., C.G.A. or C.M.A.
Architect	Baccalaureate or Licenciatura Degree; or state/provincial license[2]
Computer Systems Analyst	Baccalaureate or Licenciatura Degree; or Post−Secondary Diploma[3] or Post−Secondary Certificate[4], and three years experience
Disaster Relief Insurance Claims Adjuster (claims adjuster employed by an insurance company located in the territory of a Party, or an independent claims adjuster)	Baccalaureate or Licenciatura Degree, and successful completion of training in the appropriate areas of insurance adjustment pertaining to disaster relief claims; or three years experience in claims adjustment and successful completion of training in the appropriate areas of insurance adjustment pertaining to disaster relief claims
Economist	Baccalaureate or Licenciatura Degree
Engineer	Baccalaureate or Licenciatura Degree; or state/provincial license
Forester	Baccalaureate or Licenciatura Degree; or state/provincial license
Graphic Designer	Baccalaureate or Licenciatura Degree; or Post−Secondary Diploma or Post−Secondary Certificate, and three years experience
Hotel Manager	Baccalaureate or Licenciatura Degree in hotel/restaurant management; or Post−Secondary Diploma or Post−Secondary Certificate in hotel/restaurant management, and three years experience in hotel/restaurant management
Industrial Designer	Baccalaureate or Licenciatura Degree; or Post−Secondary Diploma or Post−Secondary Certificate, and three years experience
Interior Designer	Baccalaureate or Licenciatura Degree; or Post−Secondary Diploma or Post−Secondary Certificate, and three years experience
Land Surveyor	Baccalaureate or Licenciatura Degree; or state/provincial/federal license
Landscape Architect	Baccalaureate or Licenciatura Degree

[1] A business person seeking temporary entry under this Appendix may also perform training functions relating to the profession, including conducting seminars.
[2] "State/provincial license" and "state/provincial/federal license" mean any document issued by a state, provincial or federal government, as the case may be, or under its authority, but not by a local government, that permits a person to engage in a regulated activity or profession.
[3] "Post−Secondary Diploma" means a credential issued, on completion of two or more years of post−secondary education, by an accredited academic institution in Canada or the United States.
[4] "Post−Secondary Certificate" means a certificate issued, on completion of two or more years of post−secondary education at an academic institution, by the federal government of Mexico or a state government in Mexico, an academic institution recognized by the federal government or a state government, or an academic institution created by federal or state law.

Lawyer (including Notary in the Province of Quebec)	LL.B., J.D., LL.L., B.C.L. or Licenciatura Degree (five years); or membership in a state/provincial bar
Librarian	M.L.S. or B.L.S. (for which another Baccalaureate or Licenciatura Degree was a prerequisite)
Management Consultant	Baccalaureate or Licenciatura Degree; or equivalent professional experience as established by statement or professional credential attesting to five years experience as a management consultant, or five years experience in a field of specialty related to the consulting agreement
Mathematician (including Statistician)	Baccalaureate or Licenciatura Degree
Range Manager/Range Conservationalist	Baccalaureate or Licenciatura Degree
Research Assistant (working in a post–secondary educational institution)	Baccalaureate or Licenciatura Degree
Scientific Technician/Technologist[1]	Possession of (a) theoretical knowledge of any of the following disciplines: agricultural sciences, astronomy, biology, chemistry, engineering, forestry, geology, geophysics, meteorology or physics; and (b) the ability to solve practical problems in any of those disciplines, or the ability to apply principles of any of those disciplines to basic or applied research
Social Worker	Baccalaureate or Licenciatura Degree
Sylviculturist (including Forestry Specialist)	Baccalaureate or Licenciatura Degree
Technical Publications Writer	Baccalaureate or Licenciatura Degree; or Post–Secondary Diploma or Post–Secondary Certificate, and three years experience
Urban Planner (including Geographer)	Baccalaureate or Licenciatura Degree
Vocational Counsellor	Baccalaureate or Licenciatura Degree
Medical/Allied Professional	
Dentist	D.D.S., D.M.D., Doctor en Odontologia or Doctor en Cirugia Dental; or state/provincial license
Dietitian	Baccalaureate or Licenciatura Degree; or state/provincial license
Medical Laboratory Technologist (Canada)/Medical Technologist (Mexico and the United States)[2]	Baccalaureate or Licenciatura Degree; or Post–Secondary Diploma or Post–Secondary Certificate, and three years experience
Nutritionist	Baccalaureate or Licenciatura Degree
Occupational Therapist	Baccalaureate or Licenciatura Degree; or state/provincial license
Pharmacist	Baccalaureate or Licenciatura Degree; or state/provincial license
Physician (teaching or research only)	M.D. or Doctor en Medicina; or state/provincial license
Physiotherapist/Physical Therapist	Baccalaureate or Licenciatura Degree; or state/provincial license
Psychologist	State/provincial license; or Licenciatura Degree

[1]   A business person in this category must be seeking temporary entry to work in direct support of professionals in agricultural sciences, astronomy, biology, chemistry, engineering, forestry, geology, geophysics, meteorology or physics.
[2]   A business person in this category must be seeking temporary entry to perform in a laboratory chemical, biological, hematological, immunologic, microscopic or bacteriological tests and analyses for diagnosis, treatment or prevention of disease.

Recreational Therapist	Baccalaureate or Licenciatura Degree
Registered Nurse	State/provincial license; or Licenciatura Degree
Veterinarian	D.V.M., D.M.V. or Doctor en Veterinaria; or state/provincial license

Scientist

Agriculturist (including Agronomist)	Baccalaureate or Licenciatura Degree
Animal Breeder	Baccalaureate or Licenciatura Degree
Animal Scientist	Baccalaureate or Licenciatura Degree
Apiculturist	Baccalaureate or Licenciatura Degree
Astronomer	Baccalaureate or Licenciatura Degree
Biochemist	Baccalaureate or Licenciatura Degree
Biologist	Baccalaureate or Licenciatura Degree
Chemist	Baccalaureate or Licenciatura Degree
Dairy Scientist	Baccalaureate or Licenciatura Degree
Entomologist	Baccalaureate or Licenciatura Degree
Epidemiologist	Baccalaureate or Licenciatura Degree
Geneticist	Baccalaureate or Licenciatura Degree
Geologist	Baccalaureate or Licenciatura Degree
Geochemist	Baccalaureate or Licenciatura Degree
Geophysicist (including Oceanographer in Mexico and the United States)	Baccalaureate or Licenciatura Degree
Horticulturist	Baccalaureate or Licenciatura Degree
Meteorologist	Baccalaureate or Licenciatura Degree
Pharmacologist	Baccalaureate or Licenciatura Degree
Physicist (including Oceanographer in Canada)	Baccalaureate or Licenciatura Degree
Plant Breeder	Baccalaureate or Licenciatura Degree
Poultry Scientist	Baccalaureate or Licenciatura Degree
Soil Scientist	Baccalaureate or Licenciatura Degree
Zoologist	Baccalaureate or Licenciatura Degree

Teacher

College	Baccalaureate or Licenciatura Degree
Seminary	Baccalaureate or Licenciatura Degree
University	Baccalaureate or Licenciatura Degree

Appendix 1603.D.4
United States

1. Beginning on the date of entry into force of this Agreement as between the United States and Mexico, the United States shall annually approve as many as 5,500 initial petitions of business persons of Mexico seeking temporary entry under Section D of Annex 1603 to engage in a business activity at a professional level in a profession set out in Appendix 1603.D.1.

2. For purposes of paragraph 1, the United States shall not take into account:

   (a) the renewal of a period of temporary entry;

   (b) the entry of a spouse or children accompanying or following to join the principal business person;

    (c) an admission under section 101(a)(15)(H)(i)(b) of the *Immigration and Nationality Act*, 1952, as may be amended, including the worldwide numerical limit established by section 214(g)(1)(A) of that Act; or

    (d) an admission under any other provision of section 101(a)(15) of that Act relating to the entry of professionals.

3.   Paragraphs 4 and 5 of Section D of Annex 1603 shall apply as between the United States and Mexico for no longer than:

    (a) the period that such paragraphs or similar provisions may apply as between the United States and any other Party other than Canada or any non—Party; or

    (b) 10 years after the date of entry into force of this Agreement as between such Parties,

whichever period is shorter.

Annex 1604.2
Provision of Information

    The obligations under Article 1604(2) shall take effect with respect to Mexico one year after the date of entry into force of this Agreement.

Annex 1608
Country — Specific Definitions

For purposes of this Chapter:

citizen means, with respect to Mexico, a national or a citizen according to the existing provisions of Articles 30 and 34, respectively, of the Mexican Constitution; and

existing means, as between:

    (a) Canada and Mexico, and Mexico and the United States, in effect on the date of entry into force of this Agreement; and

    (b) Canada and the United States, in effect on January 1, 1989.

Appendix 4-C

APPENDIX A

SAMPLE OF IMM 5321 (09—94) B — APPLICATION FOR TRADER/INVESTOR STATUS

Citizenship and Immigration Canada / **Citoyenneté et Immigration Canada**

NORTH AMERICAN FREE TRADE AGREEMENT
APPLICATION FOR TRADER/INVESTOR STATUS
(EMPLOYMENT AUTHORIZATION)

ACCORD DE LIBRE-ÉCHANGE NORD AMÉRICAIN
DEMANDE DE STATUT DE NÉGOCIANT OU D'INVESTISSEUR
(PERMIS DE TRAVAIL)

A **TRADER** is a business person under Chapter 16 of the North American Free Trade Agreement (NAFTA) who is seeking temporary entry to Canada to carry on substantial trade in goods or services principally between Canada and the United States/Mexico and who will be employed in a capacity that is supervisory or executive or involves essential skills.

An **INVESTOR** is a business person under Chapter 16 of the NAFTA who is seeking temporary entry into Canada solely to develop and direct the operations of an enterprise in which the business person has invested, or is actively in the process of investing, a substantial amount of capital.

Complete only those sections that apply to the status you are seeking, i.e., Trader or Investor status. If you wish consideration under both, complete the sections applicable to both. Only if you are seeking Trader or Investor status on the basis of being an employee of a qualifying person or enterprise should you complete that section. Please read the entire application and ensure that you complete all parts that pertain to your circumstances.

Please note that a Visa or Immigration Officer must be completely satisfied that all applicable criteria are met before issuing an Employment Authorization. It is your obligation to provide sufficient supporting documentation (original documents only) that clearly shows compliance with requirements.

Un NÉGOCIANT est un homme ou une femme d'affaires visé(e) au chapitre 16 de l'ALENA qui demande à entrer temporairement au Canada pour y mener un important commerce de produits ou de services, principalement entre le Canada et les États-Unis ou le Mexique, et qui sera employé(e) en qualité de superviseur ou de directeur ou occupera un poste exigeant des compétences essentielles.

Un INVESTISSEUR est un homme ou une femme d'affaires visé(e) au chapitre 16 de l'ALENA qui demande à entrer temporairement au Canada dans le seul but d'y développer et diriger les opérations d'une entreprise dans laquelle il ou elle a investi, ou est activement en train d'investir, une somme importante.

Vous ne devez remplir que les sections qui s'apliquent au statut que vous demandez soit le statut de négociant ou d'investisseur. Si vous désirez qu'on examine votre admissibilité à la fois à l'un ou l'autre titre, veuillez remplir toutes les sections. Seul le demandeur du statut de négociant ou d'investisseur en tant qu'employé d'une personne ou entreprise admissible à ce même statut devrait remplir la section en cause. Veuillez lire le formulaire de demande au complet et prendre soin de remplir toutes les sections qui ont trait à votre cas.

Veuillez noter que l'agent des visas ou l'agent d'immigration, selon le cas, doit être tout à fait convaincu que tous les critères applicables sont respectés avant de vous délivrer un permis de travail. Il vous incombe de présenter les documents nécessaires à l'appui de votre demande (documents originaux seulement) qui établissent clairement qu'il est satisfait aux exigences.

IMM 5321 (09-94) B

Canadä

113

APPENDIX A (CONT'D)

SAMPLE OF IMM 5321 (09–94) B – APPLICATION FOR TRADER/INVESTOR STATUS

Citizenship and Immigration Canada   Citoyenneté et Immigration Canada

PROTECTED WHEN COMPLETED - B
PROTÉGÉ UNE FOIS REMPLI

NORTH AMERICAN FREE TRADE AGREEMENT
APPLICATION FOR TRADER/INVESTOR STATUS
(EMPLOYMENT AUTHORIZATION)

ACCORD DE LIBRE-ÉCHANGE NORD AMÉRICAIN
DEMANDE DE STATUT DE NÉGOCIANT OU D'INVESTISSEUR
(PERMIS DE TRAVAIL)

SECTION A - BASIC INFORMATION (To be completed by all applicants)
SECTION A - RENSEIGNEMENTS DE BASE (Doit être rempli par tous les demandeurs)

APPLICANT SURNAME - NOM DE FAMILLE DU DEMANDEUR	FIRST NAME - PRÉNOM	SECOND NAME - AUTRE NOM

ADDRESS - ADRESSE

DATE OF BIRTH / DATE DE NAISSANCE — D-J M Y-A

PLACE OF BIRTH - LIEU DE NAISSANCE

CITIZENSHIP - CITOYENNETÉ

CITIZENSHIP CERTIFICATE, BIRTH CERTIFICATE OR PASSPORT
CERTIFICAT DE CITOYENNETÉ, CERTIFICAT DE NAISSANCE OU PASSEPORT

ACCOMPANYING DEPENDANTS - PERSONNES À CHARGE ACCOMPAGNANT LE DEMANDEUR

NAME / NOM	DATE OF BIRTH / DATE DE NAISSANCE	RELATIONSHIP / LIEN DE PARENTÉ

DETAILS OF ENTERPRISE IN CANADA - DÉTAILS DE L'ENTREPRISE AU CANADA

NAME (INCLUDING OPERATING NAME) - NOM (PRÉCISEZ LE NOM COMMERCIAL)

DATE(S) AND PLACE(S) OF INCORPORATION, REGISTRATION, LICENCING OR OTHER ESTABLISHMENT OF THE BUSINESS IN CANADA
DATE(S) ET LIEU(X) DE CONSTITUTION EN SOCIÉTÉ, D'ENREGISTREMENT, D'OBTENTION DE PERMIS OU AUTRE FORME D'ACTE CONSTITUTIF DE L'ENTREPRISE AU CANADA

BUSINESS ADDRESS - ADRESSE COMMERCIALE

DESCRIBE THE TRADE OR BUSINESS ACTIVITIES OF THE ENTERPRISE
DESCRIPTION DU COMMERCE OU DES ACTIVITÉS COMMERCIALES DE L'ENTREPRISE

IMM 5321 (09-94) B

Canada

APPENDIX A (CONT'D)

SAMPLE OF IMM 5321 (09-94) B - APPLICATION FOR TRADER/INVESTOR STATUS

SECTION B - COMMON REQUIREMENTS (To be completed by all applicants)
SECTION B - CONDITIONS GÉNÉRALES (Doit être remplie par tous les demandeurs)

NATIONALITY (If the enterprise is owned by a person or persons, provide the following ownership/shareholder information)
NATIONALITÉ (Si l'entreprise appartient à une ou plusieurs personnes, veuillez fournir ci-dessous les renseignements demandés concernant les propriétaires ou actionnaires)

FULL NAME / NOM COMPLET	DATE OF BIRTH / DATE DE NAISSANCE (D-J M Y-A)	CITIZENSHIP / CITOYENNETÉ	STATUS IN CANADA / STATUT AU CANADA	AMOUNT INVESTED / SOMME INVESTIE	% OF STOCK OWNED / % DES ACTIONS DÉTENUES

IF THE ENTERPRISE IS OWNED BY AN ESTABLISHED FIRM OR FIRMS (JOINT OWNERSHIP BY MAXIMUM OF TWO FIRMS), PROVIDE THE FOLLOWING OWNERSHIP INFORMATION
SI L'ENTREPRISE EST LA PROPRIÉTÉ D'UNE OU PLUSIEURS FIRMES ÉTABLIES (MAXIMUM DE DEUX FIRMES), VEUILLEZ FOURNIR LES RENSEIGNEMENTS DEMANDÉS CI-DESSOUS

NAME OF OWNING FIRM - NOM DE LA FIRME PROPRIÉTAIRE	ADDRESS - ADRESSE

TYPE OF BUSINESS - GENRE D'ENTREPRISE	PERCENTAGE OF OWNERSHIP OF OWNING FIRM(S) IN ENTERPRISE / POURCENTAGE DE LA PARTICIPATION DE LA(DES) FIRME(S) PROPRIÉTAIRE(S) DANS L'ENTREPRISE ▶ %	%

FULL NAME OF SHAREHOLDER / NOM COMPLET DE L'ACTIONNAIRE	DATE OF BIRTH / DATE DE NAISSANCE (D-J M Y-A)	CITIZENSHIP / CITOYENNETÉ	INDICATE IF PERMANENT RESIDENT OF CANADA / INDIQUER SI RÉSIDENT PERMANENT AU CANADA		% OF STOCK OWNED / % DES ACTIONS DÉTENUES
			☐ YES / OUI	☐ NO / NON	
			☐ YES / OUI	☐ NO / NON	
			☐ YES / OUI	☐ NO / NON	
			☐ YES / OUI	☐ NO / NON	
			☐ YES / OUI	☐ NO / NON	

SECTION C - TRADER REQUIREMENTS (To be completed only if applying for Trader status)
SECTION C - EXIGENCES RELATIVES AU STATUT DE NÉGOCIANT (À remplir par les demandeurs du statut de négociant)

1. **EVIDENCE THAT THE POSITION IS EXECUTIVE OR SUPERVISORY OR REQUIRES ESSENTIAL SKILLS**
(Complete only those sections which apply)
PREUVES QUE LE POSTE EST UN POSTE DE DIRECTEUR OU DE SUPERVISEUR OU UN POSTE EXIGEANT DES COMPÉTENCES ESSENTIELLES (Ne remplissez que les parties applicables)

JOB TITLE - TITRE DU POSTE	SALARY - SALAIRE	INDICATE LOCATION OF JOB POSITION IN ORGANIZATIONAL STRUCTURE / INDIQUEZ OÙ SE SITUE LE POSTE DANS LA STRUCTURE ORGANISATIONNELLE

JOB DUTIES - FONCTIONS DU POSTE

APPENDIX A (CONT'D)
SAMPLE OF IMM 5321 (09—94) B — APPLICATION FOR TRADER/INVESTOR STATUS

DESCRIBE DEGREE OF ULTIMATE CONTROL AND RESPONSIBILITY OVER OPERATIONS
PRÉCISEZ LE DEGRÉ DE CONTRÔLE ET DE RESPONSABILITÉ ULTIMES DES OPÉRATIONS

HOW MANY EMPLOYEES AND WHAT JOB TITLES REPORT DIRECTLY TO THIS POSITION?
COMBIEN D'EMPLOYÉS RELÈVENT DIRECTEMENT DE CE POSTE ET QUELS SONT LEURS TITRES?

WHAT EXECUTIVE OR SUPERVISORY EXPERIENCE IS REQUIRED FOR THIS JOB?
QUELLE EXPÉRIENCE À TITRE DE DIRECTEUR OU DE SUPERVISEUR EXIGE LE POSTE EN QUESTION?

IF THE JOB IS NEITHER EXECUTIVE NOR SUPERVISORY BUT REQUIRES ESSENTIAL SKILLS, DESCRIBE IN DETAIL WHAT ESSENTIAL SKILLS ARE REQUIRED. (ESSENTIAL SKILLS ARE SPECIAL QUALIFICATIONS WHICH ARE ABSOLUTELY NECESSARY FOR THE EFFECTIVE OPERATION OF THE FIRM IN CANADA OVER AND ABOVE QUALIFICATIONS OF AN ORDINARY SKILLED WORKER)
SI LE POSTE N'EST PAS CELUI DE DIRECTEUR OU DE SUPERVISEUR MAIS QU'IL EXIGE DES COMPÉTENCES ESSENTIELLES, EXPLIQUEZ DE QUELLES COMPÉTENCES IL S'AGIT. (LES COMPÉTENCES ESSENTIELLES SONT LES QUALITÉS SPÉCIALES QUI SONT ABSOLUMENT NÉCESSAIRES POUR ASSURER L'EFFICACITÉ DES OPÉRATIONS CANADIENNES DE L'ENTREPRISE ET QUE N'A PAS LE TRAVAILLEUR SPÉCIALISÉ ORDINAIRE.)

2. **EVIDENCE THAT THE FIRM'S ACTIVITIES CONSTITUTE TRADE**
The term "TRADE" means the exchange, purchase, or sale of goods and/or services. Goods are tangible commodities or merchandise having intrinsic value, excluding money, securities and negotiable instruments. Services are economic activities whose outputs are other than tangible goods (i.e., international banking, insurance, transportation, communications and data processing, advertising, accounting, design and engineering, management consulting, tourism, etc.).

List the documents you will provide to show exchange / purchase / sale of goods and / or services:

PREUVES QUE LES ACTIVITÉS DE L'ENTREPRISE ONT VALEUR DE COMMERCE
Le terme "COMMERCE" s'entend de l'échange, de l'achat ou de la vente de produits ou de services. Les produits sont des articles ou des marchandises tangibles ayant une valeur intrinsèque, à l'exception de l'argent, des titres et des effets négociables. Les services sont des activités économiques dont les résultats ne sont pas des produits tangibles. Au nombre de ces activités figurent, entre autres, les services bancaires internationaux, les assurances, le transport, les communications et le traitement des données, la publicité, la comptabilité, la conception et l'ingénierie, les services de conseil et le tourisme.

Énumérez les documents que vous fournissez à titre de preuve de l'échange, de l'achat ou de la vente de produits ou de services :

APPENDIX 4-C

APPENDIX A (CONT'D)

SAMPLE OF IMM 5321 (09-94) B – APPLICATION FOR TRADER/INVESTOR STATUS

3. EVIDENCE THAT THE TRADE IS PRINCIPALLY BETWEEN CANADA AND THE UNITED STATES/MEXICO

OVER 50% OF THE TOTAL VOLUME OF TRADE CONDUCTED IN CANADA BY THE FIRM'S CANADIAN OFFICE MUST BE BETWEEN CANADA AND THE UNITED STATES/MEXICO.

PREUVES QUE LE COMMERCE SE FAIT PRINCIPALEMENT ENTRE LE CANADA ET LES ÉTATS-UNIS OU LE MEXIQUE

PLUS DE 50% DU VOLUME TOTAL DU COMMERCE MENÉ AU CANADA PAR LA SUCCURSALE CANADIENNE DE L'ENTREPRISE DOIT L'ÊTRE ENTRE LE CANADA ET LES ÉTATS-UNIS OU LE MEXIQUE.

CALENDAR YEAR *ANNÉE CIVILE*	TOTAL TRADE OR BUSINESS CONDUCTED BY THE ENTERPRISE IN CANADA *VALEUR TOTALE DU COMMERCE OU DES AFFAIRES DE L'ENTREPRISE AU CANADA* (CANADIAN DOLLARS) *(EN DOLLAR CANADIEN)*	THE APPROXIMATE NUMBER OF SEPARATE BUSINESS TRANSACTIONS THIS REPRESENTS *LE NOMBRE APPROXIMATIF DE TRANSACTIONS COMMERCIALES DISTINCTES QUE CETTE SOMME REPRÉSENTE*

BREAKDOWN OF TRADE: - *RÉPARTITION DU COMMERCE:*

VALUE OF TRANSACTIONS BETWEEN CANADA AND U.S./MEXICO
VALEUR DES TRANSACTIONS ENTRE LE CANADA ET LES ÉTATS-UNIS OU LE MEXIQUE _____ (CANADIAN DOLLARS) *(EN DOLLAR CANADIEN)*

NUMBER OF TRANSACTIONS
NOMBRE DE TRANSACTIONS

VALUE OF "IN CANADA" TRANSACTIONS
VALEUR DES TRANSACTIONS "AU CANADA" _____ (CANADIAN DOLLARS) *(EN DOLLAR CANADIEN)*

NUMBER OF TRANSACTIONS
NOMBRE DE TRANSACTIONS

VALUE OF TRANSACTIONS BETWEEN CANADA AND COUNTRIES OTHER THAN U.S./MEXICO
VALEUR DES TRANSACTIONS ENTRE LE CANADA ET DES PAYS AUTRES QUE LES ÉTATS-UNIS OU LE MEXIQUE _____ (CANADIAN DOLLARS) *(EN DOLLAR CANADIEN)*

NUMBER OF TRANSACTIONS
NOMBRE DE TRANSACTIONS

SECTION D - INVESTOR REQUIREMENTS (To be completed only if applying for investor status)
SECTION D - EXIGENCES RELATIVES AU STATUT D'INVESTISSEUR (À remplir par les demandeurs du statut d'investisseur)

1. EVIDENCE THAT THE INVESTMENT IS SUBSTANTIAL
PREUVE QUE L'INVESTISSEMENT EST IMPORTANT

IF YOU ARE INVESTING IN AN EXISTING BUSINESS:
SI VOUS INVESTISSEZ DANS UNE ENTREPRISE EXISTANTE:

WHAT IS THE ESTABLISHED WORTH OF THE BUSINESS?
QUELLE EST LA VALEUR ÉTABLIE DE L'ENTREPRISE? _____ (CANADIAN DOLLARS) *(EN DOLLAR CANADIEN)*

WHAT IS THE BREAKDOWN OF THE ESTABLISHED WORTH (E.G., LAND, BUILDING, EQUIPMENT, INVENTORY, ETC.)?
COMMENT SE RÉPARTIT LA VALEUR ÉTABLIE (SOIT ENTRE LE TERRAIN, L'IMMEUBLE, L'ÉQUIPEMENT, L'INVENTAIRE, ETC.)?

_____ _____ (CANADIAN DOLLARS) *(EN DOLLAR CANADIEN)*

_____ _____ (CANADIAN DOLLARS) *(EN DOLLAR CANADIEN)*

_____ _____ (CANADIAN DOLLARS) *(EN DOLLAR CANADIEN)*

_____ _____ (CANADIAN DOLLARS) *(EN DOLLAR CANADIEN)*

_____ _____ (CANADIAN DOLLARS) *(EN DOLLAR CANADIEN)*

WHAT DOCUMENTS ARE YOU ATTACHING WHICH CONFIRM THE ESTABLISHED WORTH?
QUELS DOCUMENTS JOIGNEZ-VOUS À TITRE DE CONFIRMATION DE LA VALEUR ÉTABLIE?

WHAT AMOUNT ARE YOU INVESTING? _____ (CANADIAN DOLLARS) THIS AMOUNT REPRESENTS PER CENT OF THE ESTABLISHED WORTH
À COMBIEN SE CHIFFRE VOTRE INVESTISSEMENT? *(EN DOLLAR CANADIEN)* *CETTE SOMME REPRÉSENTE* _____ *P. 100 DE LA VALEUR ÉTABLIE*

IF YOU ARE INVESTING IN A NEW BUSINESS:
SI VOUS INVESTISSEZ DANS UNE NOUVELLE ENTREPRISE:

WHAT IS THE TOTAL AMOUNT OF MONEY NECESSARY TO ESTABLISH THE ENTERPRISE?
QUELLE SOMME TOTALE EST NÉCESSAIRE POUR ÉTABLIR L'ENTREPRISE? _____ (CANADIAN DOLLARS) *(EN DOLLAR CANADIEN)*

DESCRIBE HOW YOU ARRIVED AT THIS FIGURE
EXPLIQUEZ COMMENT VOUS ÊTES ARRIVÉ À CE CHIFFRE

WHAT AMOUNT ARE YOU INVESTING? _____ (CANADIAN DOLLARS) THIS AMOUNT REPRESENTS PER CENT OF THE ESTABLISHED WORTH
À COMBIEN SE CHIFFRE VOTRE INVESTISSEMENT? *(EN DOLLAR CANADIEN)* *CETTE SOMME REPRÉSENTE* _____ *P. 100 DE LA VALEUR ÉTABLIE*

APPENDIX A (CONT'D)
SAMPLE OF IMM 5321 (09–94) B – APPLICATION FOR TRADER/INVESTOR STATUS

2. **EVIDENCE THAT FUNDS HAVE BEEN OR WILL BE INVESTED**
   PREUVES QU'UNE SOMME A ÉTÉ OU SERA INVESTIE

LIST THE DOCUMENTS BEING PROVIDED WHICH SHOW THAT FUNDS EITHER HAVE BEEN INVESTED OR HAVE BEEN IRREVOCABLY COMMITTED FOR INVESTMENT.
ÉNUMÉREZ LES DOCUMENTS JOINTS POUR ÉTABLIR QUE DES FONDS ONT ÉTÉ INVESTIS OU IRRÉVOCABLEMENT ENGAGÉS À TITRE D'INVESTISSEMENT.

LIST THE DOCUMENTS BEING PROVIDED WHICH SHOW THE PERSON OR FIRM MAKING THE INVESTMENT HAS HAD POSSESSION AND CONTROL OF THE FUNDS OR OTHER CAPITAL ASSETS BEING USED FOR THE INVESTMENT.
ÉNUMÉREZ LES DOCUMENTS JOINTS POUR ÉTABLIR QUE LES FONDS OU AUTRES BIENS INVESTIS APPARTIENNENT EN PROPRE À LA PERSONNE OU À LA FIRME QUI FAIT L'INVESTISSEMENT.

DESCRIBE AND DOCUMENT THE VARIOUS FORMS OF INVESTMENT UTILIZED, I.E., CASH, EQUIPMENT, PURCHASES, INVENTORY, INDEBTEDNESS, LEASE / RENT PAYMENTS, ETC.
ÉNUMÉREZ ET PRÉCISEZ LES DIVERSES FORMES D'INVESTISSEMENT EN CAUSE: ARGENT COMPTANT, ÉQUIPEMENT, ACHATS, STOCKS, ENDETTEMENT, PAIEMENTS DE LOYER, ETC.

3. **EVIDENCE THAT THE ENTREPRISE IS REAL AND COMMERCIAL**
   PREUVES QUE L'ENTREPRISE EST RÉELLE ET ACTIVE

THE ENTERPRISE MUST BE A REAL AND ACTIVE COMMERCIAL ENTREPRENEURIAL UNDERTAKING WHICH OPERATES CONTINUOUSLY TO PRODUCE SOME SERVICE OR COMMODITY FOR PROFIT. A PLAN FOR FUTURE INVESTMENT, EXPANSION, AND / OR DEVELOPMENT WILL ASSIST THE CONSULATE IN DETERMINING THE VIABILITY OF THE COMMERCIAL ENTERPRISE. LIST THE DOCUMENTS BEING PROVIDED TO SHOW COMPLIANCE WITH THIS CRITERION.
L'ENTREPRISE DOIT ÊTRE UNE ENTITÉ OU UNE EXPLOITATION COMMERCIALE RÉELLE OU ACTIVE, QUI FONCTIONNE DE FAÇON CONTINUE ET PRODUIT QUELQUE SERVICE OU ARTICLE DANS UN BUT LUCRATIF. UN PLAN D'INVESTISSEMENT, D'AGRANDISSEMENT ET(OU) D'EXPANSION AIDERA L'AGENT DES VISAS À APPRÉCIER LA VIABILITÉ DE L'ENTREPRISE. ÉNUMÉREZ LES DOCUMENTS JOINTS POUR ÉTABLIR QU'IL EST SATISFAIT À CE CRITÈRE.

APPENDIX 4-C

TEMPORARY ENTRY OF BUSINESS PERSONS
NORTH AMERICAN FREE TRADE AGREEMENT (NAFTA)

APPENDIX A (CONT'D)
SAMPLE OF IMM 5321 (09—94) B — APPLICATION FOR TRADER/INVESTOR STATUS

---

4. EVIDENCE THAT THE INVESTMENT IS MORE THAN MARGINAL
PREUVES QUE L'INVESTISSEMENT EST PLUS QUE MARGINAL

WHAT IS THE ANTICIPATED AMOUNT OF NET INCOME TO BE GENERATED OVER THE NEXT YEAR BY THE INVESTMENT?
QUEL EST LE MONTANT PRÉVU DE REVENU NET QUE PROCURERA L'INVESTISSEMENT AU COURS DE L'ANNÉE À VENIR?

(CANADIAN DOLLARS)
(EN DOLLAR CANADIEN)

DESCRIBE HOW YOU ARRIVED AT THIS FIGURE.
EXPLIQUEZ COMMENT VOUS ÊTES ARRIVÉ À CE CHIFFRE.

DESCRIBE HOW THE INVESTMENT WILL MAINTAIN OR EXPAND JOB OPPORTUNITIES LOCALLY.
DÉCRIVEZ COMMENT L'INVESTISSEMENT PERMETTRA DE MAINTENIR OU DE CRÉER DES EMPLOIS LOCALEMENT.

---

5. EVIDENCE THAT YOU PLAN TO "DEVELOP AND DIRECT" THE ENTERPRISE
PREUVES QUE VOUS PLANIFIEZ "DÉVELOPPER ET DIRIGER" L'ENTREPRISE

DESCRIBE HOW YOUR POSITION WILL ALLOW YOU TO "DEVELOP AND DIRECT" THE ENTERPRISE (I.E., EXERCISE OPERATIONAL AND / OR CORPORATE CONTROL). IF YOU, OR THE AMERICAN/MEXICAN FIRM, HAVE LESS THAN 50 PER CENT CONTROLLING INTEREST IN THE CANADIAN ENTERPRISE, YOU MUST BE ABLE TO DEMONSTRATE HOW, IN EFFECT, OPERATIONAL CONTROL WILL BE ACHIEVED.
DÉCRIVEZ COMMENT VOTRE POSTE VOUS PERMETTRA DE "DÉVELOPPER ET DIRIGER" L'ENTREPRISE (C'EST-À-DIRE EXERCER LE CONTRÔLE OPÉRATIONNEL OU LA DIRECTION DE L'ENTREPRISE). SI VOTRE PARTICIPATION OU CELLE DE LA FIRME AMÉRICAINE OU MEXICAINE DANS L'ENTREPRISE CANADIENNE EST INFÉRIEURE À 50 P. 100, VOUS DEVEZ POUVOIR EXPLIQUER COMMENT, EN RÉALITÉ, VOUS EXERCEREZ LE CONTRÔLE OPÉRATIONNEL.

APPENDIX A (CONT'D)

SAMPLE OF IMM 5321 (09–94) B – APPLICATION FOR TRADER/INVESTOR STATUS

SECTION E APPLICANT SEEKING STATUS AS AN EMPLOYEE OF A TRADER OR INVESTOR

EMPLOYER STATUS: IN ORDER TO QUALIFY TO BRING AN EMPLOYEE TO CANADA IN TRADER OR INVESTOR STATUS, THE EMPLOYER MUST ALREADY HOLD TRADER OR INVESTOR STATUS IN CANADA. WHERE THE PROSPECTIVE EMPLOYER IS A CORPORATION OR OTHER BUSINESS ORGANIZATION, THE EMPLOYER MUST BE RESIDING IN THE UNITED STATES/MEXICO IF NOT MAINTAINING STATUS IN CANADA. IF YOU ARE AN EMPLOYEE, YOUR EMPLOYER MUST SUPPORT THIS APPLICATION WITH EVIDENCE OF TRADER OR INVESTOR STATUS IN CANADA, OR OF RESIDENCE IN THE UNITED STATES/MEXICO.

PROVIDE FULL PARTICULARS OF YOUR QUALIFICATIONS TO PERFORM IN AN EXECUTIVE OR SUPERVISORY POSITION. IF THE JOB IS ONE REQUIRING ESSENTIAL KNOWLEDGE OR SKILLS, DESCRIBE HOW YOU HAVE COME TO POSSESS THE ESSENTIAL SPECIALIZATION (I.E., COMMENT ON THE UNIQUENESS OF YOUR SKILLS AND THE PERIOD OF TRAINING REQUIRED TO PERFORM THE CONTEMPLATED JOB DUTIES. YOU MAY WISH TO ATTACH A CURRICULUM VITAE. IF YOU ARE NOT IN THE EXECUTIVE / SUPERVISORY / ESSENTIAL KNOWLEDGE CATEGORY AND ARE SEEKING ENTRY AS A HIGHLY TRAINED TECHNICIAN, PROVIDE FULL DETAILS OF YOUR TRAINING AND EXPERIENCE. (FOR APPLICANTS SEEKING ENTRY FOR POSITIONS REQUIRING ESSENTIAL SKILLS OR WHO ARE HIGHLY TRAINED TECHNICIANS, EMPLOYERS WILL HAVE TO PROVIDE EVIDENCE THAT ESSENTIAL OR HIGH-LEVEL SKILLS ARE REQUIRED.) INVESTOR STATUS CAN ALSO BE GRANTED FOR A ONE YEAR PERIOD TO AN EMPLOYEE WHO IS FAMILIAR WITH AN AMERICAN/A MEXICAN FIRM FOR THE PURPOSE OF STARTING-UP A CANADIAN AFFILIATE OF THAT FIRM.

SECTION E DEMANDEUR DE STATUT À TITRE D'EMPLOYÉ D'UN NÉGOCIANT OU D'UN INVESTISSEUR

STATUT DE L'EMPLOYEUR: POUR ÊTRE AUTORISÉ À FAIRE VENIR UN EMPLOYÉ AU CANADA EN QUALITÉ DE NÉGOCIANT OU D'INVESTISSEUR, L'EMPLOYEUR DOIT DÉJÀ AVOIR CE STATUT AU CANADA. SI L'EMPLOYEUR ÉVENTUEL EST UNE SOCIÉTÉ OU AUTRE ORGANISATION COMMERCIALE, L'EMPLOYEUR DOIT ÊTRE UN RÉSIDENT DES ÉTATS-UNIS OU DU MEXIQUE S'IL N'A PAS CE STATUT AU CANADA. SI VOUS ÊTES UN EMPLOYÉ, VOTRE EMPLOYEUR DOIT FOURNIR À L'APPUI DE VOTRE DEMANDE UNE PREUVE SOIT DE STATUT DE NÉGOCIANT OU D'INVESTISSEUR AU CANADA, SOIT DE STATUT DE RÉSIDENT AUX ÉTATS-UNIS OU AU MEXIQUE.

VEUILLEZ FOURNIR DES DÉTAILS COMPLETS DE VOTRE QUALITÉ DE DIRECTEUR OU DE SUPERVISEUR. SI LE POSTE EXIGE DES CONNAISSANCES OU COMPÉTENCES ESSENTIELLES, DÉCRIVEZ COMMENT VOUS AVEZ ACQUIS CES DERNIÈRES (C'EST-À-DIRE EXPLIQUEZ L'UNICITÉ DE VOS COMPÉTENCES ET LA PÉRIODE DE FORMATION REQUISE POUR POUVOIR REMPLIR LES FONCTIONS ENVISAGÉES). VOUS POUVEZ, SI VOUS LE VOULEZ, JOINDRE UN CURRICULUM VITAE. SI VOUS N'ÊTES PAS UN DIRECTEUR, UN SUPERVISEUR OU UNE PERSONNE AYANT DES CONNAISSANCES ESSENTIELLES ET QUE VOUS DEMANDEZ UNE AUTORISATION DE SÉJOUR À TITRE DE TECHNICIEN DE FORMATION POUSSÉE, VEUILLEZ FOURNIR DES DÉTAILS COMPLETS DE VOTRE FORMATION ET DE VOTRE EXPÉRIENCE. (DANS LE CAS DU DEMANDEUR QUI SOLLICITE UNE AUTORISATION DE SÉJOUR EN VUE D'OCCUPER UN POSTE EXIGEANT DES COMPÉTENCES ESSENTIELLES OU QUI EST UN TECHNICIEN DE FORMATION POUSSÉE, L'EMPLOYEUR DOIT FOURNIR LA PREUVE QUE LES COMPÉTENCES ESSENTIELLES OU POUSSÉES SONT NÉCESSAIRES.) LE STATUT D'INVESTISSEUR PEUT ÉGALEMENT ÊTRE ACCORDÉ POUR UNE PÉRIODE D'UNE ANNÉE À UN EMPLOYÉ QUI CONNAÎT BIEN UNE FIRME AMÉRICAINE OU MEXICAINE EN VUE D'ÉTABLIR UNE SUCCURSALE AU CANADA.

SECTION F - PLEASE USE THIS SPACE TO PROVIDE OTHER INFORMATION WHICH YOU DEEM RELEVANT TO YOUR APPLICATION:
SECTION F - VEUILLEZ UTILISER CET ESPACE POUR FOURNIR D'AUTRES RENSEIGNEMENTS QUE VOUS JUGEZ PERTINENTS :

I AFFIRM THAT THE INFORMATION PROVIDED ON THIS FORM OR OTHERWISE PROVIDED IN THE WAY OF SUPPORTING DOCUMENTATION, WHETHER IT IS PROVIDED BY ME OR ANOTHER PERSON, IS TRUE AND COMPLETE.

LES RENSEIGNEMENTS FOURNIS DANS LE PRÉSENT FORMULAIRE ET DANS LES DOCUMENTS JUSTIFICATIFS JOINTS SONT VÉRIDIQUES, EXACTS ET COMPLETS.

_____
SIGNATURE OF APPLICANT - SIGNATURE DU DEMANDEUR

_____
DATE

THE INFORMATION YOU PROVIDE ON THIS DOCUMENT IS COLLECTED UNDER THE AUTHORITY OF THE IMMIGRATION ACT TO DETERMINE IF YOU MAY BE ADMITTED TO CANADA AS A TRADER OR AN INVESTOR. THIS INFORMATION WILL BE STORED IN PERSONAL INFORMATION BANK NUMBER CIC PPU 295, TEMPORARY WORKER RECORDS AND CASE FILE. IT IS PROTECTED AND YOU HAVE THE RIGHT OF ACCESS TO IT UNDER THE PROVISIONS OF THE PRIVACY ACT.
LES RENSEIGNEMENTS CONSIGNÉS DANS CE FORMULAIRE SONT RECUEILLIS EN VERTU DE LA LOI SUR L'IMMIGRATION AFIN DE DÉTERMINER SI VOUS POUVEZ ÊTRE ADMIS AU CANADA À TITRE DE NÉGOCIANT OU D'INVESTISSEUR. CES RENSEIGNEMENTS SERONT VERSÉS AU FICHIER DE RENSEIGNEMENTS PERSONNELS CIC PPU 295, DOSSIER ET FICHIER DES TRAVAILLEURS TEMPORAIRES. ILS SONT PROTÉGÉS ET ACCESSIBLES EN VERTU DES DISPOSITIONS DE LA LOI SUR LA PROTECTION DES RENSEIGNEMENTS PERSONNELS.

5[1]

THE GENERAL AGREEMENT ON TRADE IN SERVICES

5.1 INTRODUCTION

The General Agreement on Trade in Services ("GATS"), one of three components to the Agreement Establishing the World Trade Organization ("AEWTO") promulgated on January 1, 1995, provides expedited and simplified entry procedures for admission to Canada for business purposes and employment for individuals from 122 countries. The temporary entry provisions of the GATS consist of Annex 1B (to the World Trade Agreement) which sets out Canada's commitments, the economic sectors and/or services to which the Agreement applies, and the member Nations.

The most valuable feature of the GATS is simply that qualification of a foreign worker under its provisions permits entry into Canada *without* a job validation or foreign worker record, from the Canada Employment Centre.

The GATS provisions are in many respects similar in substance to those of the North American Free Trade Agreement ("NAFTA"), yet because they apply to individuals from more than 122 member nations, they have a much broader application. Like the NAFTA, the GATS expands but does not replace the general provisions of the *Immigration Act* pertaining to foreign workers. However, in most instances, where U.S. or Mexican nationals are concerned, the most simple course of action would be to first consider the applicability of the NAFTA before turning to the provisions of the GATS.

5.2 QUALIFICATION REQUIREMENTS

5.2.1 CITIZENSHIP AND RESIDENCE

- In order to qualify under the GATS, the applicant must be a citizen of and resident in a member nation listed in Ap-

---

1   Co-authored by Nan Berezowski.

pendix A to Annex 1B of the AEWTO (reproduced as Appendix 5-A to this chapter).

- The member nation need not be the same for both aspects of this qualification to be satisfied *(i.e., the applicant may qualify as a citizen of one nation and as a resident of another nation, so long as both nations are member nations for purposes of the GATS).*

The GATS contains an additional provision which would qualify business persons who have been accorded permanent resident status in a member nation listed in Appendix B to Annex 1B of the AEWTO (reproduced as Appendix 5-B to this chapter). To date, however, no nations have agreed to provide these reciprocal benefits and, consequently, there are no nations listed in Appendix B.

5.2.2 BUSINESS ACTIVITY

The GATS applies to a select segment of the labour market. Foreign business persons must be employed within a major service sector listed in Appendix C to Annex 1B (reproduced as Appendix 5-C to this chapter). Persons entering Canada to engage in many of the activities listed under each of the services enumerated below have not previously enjoyed access to Canada—the value of expedited and simplified procedures for gaining entry is therefore considerable.

- To qualify under the GATS, prospective applicants must be entering Canada to engage in a business activity in one of the following sectors which are defined in greater detail in Appendix 5-C to this chapter:

  ○ Business Services

  ○ Communications Services

  ○ Construction Services

  ○ Distribution Services

  ○ Environmental Services

  ○ Financial Services

  ○ Tourism and Travel Related Services

○ Transport Service

- It is important to ensure that the specific occupational services relating to the applicant are enumerated. *For example, legal, accounting and engineering personnel are found under the Business Services section, while Communication Services has the largest listing of computer related services.*

5.2.3 COMPLIANCE WITH THE *IMMIGRATION ACT*

The GATS provides specific categories under which temporary entry to Canada is facilitated; however, it does not override the general provisions pertaining to admissibility set out in section 19 of the *Immigration Act (Act)*.

- It should be ascertained whether the applicant is likely to fall within the scope of section 19 of the *Act* (criminal inadmissibility) at the onset, as such an applicant must obtain the appropriate permission to enter Canada in order to qualify for issuance of an employment authorization.

5.2.4 MIGRATION CATEGORIES

Three types of business persons qualify for admission under the GATS:

1. Business Visitors
2. Intra-company Transferees
3. Professionals

These categories will be discussed in detail below.

5.3 THE BUSINESS VISITOR (ENTRY UNDER SECTION 19(1)(h) OF THE *IMMIGRATION REGULATIONS*)

5.3.1 DEFINITION

''Business visitors'' under the GATS are citizens of a member nation (see Appendix 5-A) who will stay in Canada without obtaining remuneration from within Canada and without engaging in making direct sales to the general public or supplying services, for the purpose of participating in business meetings, business contacts, including negotiations for the sale of services and/or other similar activities including those to prepare for establishing a commercial presence in Canada.

5.3.2 REQUIREMENTS

(a) Service Supplier

- The service provider must be located in a member nation.

(b) Remuneration Outside of Canada

- The applicant must not be remunerated by the Canadian enterprise as visitor status does not permit entry where there is remuneration from a Canadian source or employer.

(c) Range of Activities

Business visitors qualifying under the GATS are not permitted to engage in employment for or on behalf of a Canadian employer. Business visitors are entitled to pursue activities which relate to the sale of services including participation in the start-up of a business in Canada.

- The applicant's activities must be limited to business meetings, negotiations and other types of business contacts. Otherwise, the applicant may not qualify as a business visitor.

5.3.3 THE APPLICATION PROCESS

- An application made for business visitor status under the GATS may be submitted at the port of entry if the foreign worker does not need a visa to travel to Canada. If the applicant requires a visa to travel to Canada, the application must be submitted to a visa office abroad.

Business visitors will be granted entry to Canada pursuant to section 19(1)(h) of the *Immigration Regulations (Regulations)* which have been amended to include sellers of services in addition to sellers of goods. Accordingly, GATS applicants can expect to be treated in the same manner as any other sellers of goods and services because the regulation does not contain any reference to the applicants' nationality.

Applications made pursuant to the business visitor category may be considered at the port of entry in the manner described in Chapter 2 relating to section 19(1) of the *Regulations*.

5.4 INTRA-COMPANY TRANSFEREES (ENTRY UNDER SECTION 20(5)(b)(i) OF THE *REGULATIONS*)

The intra-company provisions under GATS significantly expand the accessibility to the Canadian labour market of key personnel needed to oversee the Canadian operations of foreign service providers. This category is the most generous of the three categories in the GATS.

5.4.1 DEFINITION OF AN INTRA-COMPANY TRANSFEREE

"Intra-company transferees" are persons of another member nation who have been employed for a period of not less than one year and who seek temporary entry in order to render services to the same company which is engaged in substantive business operations in Canada, or a company constituted in Canada and engaged in substantive business operations in Canada and which is owned by or controlled by or affiliated with the aforementioned company.

5.4.2 THE REQUIREMENTS FOR ADMISSION OF INTRA-COMPANY TRANSFEREES

- The GATS sets out three specifically defined types of foreign workers who may qualify: senior executives, senior managers and specialists may be transferred to Canada by a foreign enterprise which is related (parent, subsidiary or affiliate) to the Canadian transferee enterprise.

   ○ As the Code E15 Job Validation exemption (see Chapter 6) applies to citizens of all nations and its terms are

generally more favourable to senior executive and manager intra-company transferees, the Code E15 Job Validation exemption should generally be utilized for these
individuals.

○ The use of the intra-company transferee provisions of
the GATS should generally be restricted to intra-company transferees whose applications are based on their
specialized knowledge.

• To qualify under the intra-company transferee category, a
foreign worker must have been employed with the related
transferor corporation in a similar position for at least one
year immediately prior to the date of the application.

In contrast, the intra-company transferee provisions of the NAFTA require that the
one year of experience must have been obtained within the three-year period immediately preceding the applicant's transfer to Canada.

(a) Executives

Executives do not generally perform duties necessary to the actual delivery of a
service. Rather, executives are responsible for overseeing, directing and controlling
the operation or enterprise. It is not an applicant's title but rather her or his actual
responsibilities that will be considered by immigration officials.

• That the applicant is an executive is determined by considering whether she or he is an individual who is primarily
responsible for:

○ the direct management of the company, establishing its
goals and policies; or

○ a major component or function of the company, and has
a wide decision-making power subject to minimal more
senior supervision.

(b) Managers

Managers must not be involved in the actual delivery of a service. For example,
performing a service, such as an accountant or architect would, will not satisfy the

requirement that executive or managerial duties be undertaken in Canada. Moreover, front line supervisors do not qualify unless the employees supervised by that person are professionals.

- Determine whether the applicant is a manager by considering whether she or he:

  ○ is responsible for directing the enterprise, or department or subdivision of the company, supervising the work of other supervisory, professional or managerial employees;

  ○ has discretionary control of the daily affairs of the company; and

  ○ has the ability to make personnel decisions.

(c) Specialists

Specialists possess an advanced level of expertise and proprietary knowledge of the enterprise's product, service, research, equipment, techniques or management.

- Admittance under the GATS specialized knowledge provisions does not discharge the applicant or the Canadian employer from the responsibility of ensuring that any Canadian licensing, registration or certification requirements are met before commencement of employment.

- To qualify under the specialized knowledge provisions, the Canadian enterprise must demonstrate that the foreign worker possesses an advanced level of knowledge and expertise of a nature so as to be critical to the well-being of the enterprise in Canada.

- This knowledge must not be readily available in Canada.

  ○ The employer's supporting letter should address this issue by stating its reasons for concluding that the applicant's specialized knowledge is not available in Canada.

○ It is not, however, necessary for the employer to make representations regarding recruitment efforts made through advertising or other means, nor do the job validation procedures apply.

The GATS requires that applicants possess ''an advanced level of expertise'' in certain aspects of the enterprise. In contrast, the NAFTA requires advanced expertise only if the transferee's application is based on knowledge of the Canadian enterprise's process and procedures.

- Under the NAFTA, if the application is based on the transferee's knowledge of the Canadian enterprise's product, service, research, equipment, techniques, management or other interests, the transferee's knowledge need only meet the standard of "specialized knowledge".

- Given that the GATS threshold of an "advanced level of expertise" is considerably higher than the specialized knowledge requirements of the NAFTA, an examination of the applicant's knowledge in relation to the Canadian employer's needs is required.

○ Note also that the specialized knowledge may apply to "other interests" of the Canadian enterprise under the NAFTA but not under the GATS.

5.4.3 THE REQUIREMENTS OF THE BUSINESS ENTERPRISE

(a) Definition of Business Enterprise

The ''business enterprise'' is referred to in the text of the GATS as a ''Juridical person'' and is defined as:

> Any legal entity duly constituted or otherwise organized under applicable law, whether for profit or otherwise, and whether privately-owned or governmentally-owned, including any corporation, trust, partnership, joint venture, sole proprietorship or association.

(b) A Substantive Business Operation

- Both the foreign and the Canadian enterprises must be engaged in a substantive business operation which corresponds to a service sector referred to in Appendix 5-C.

- The Canadian office must be of real substance having business activities which would require and utilize the executive or management functions of the foreign worker.

- The Canadian enterprise must be "doing business" defined as providing services on a regular, systematic and continuous basis. *The mere presence of an agent or office in either the member nation or Canada does not constitute "doing business" within the meaning of the GATS.*

(c) The "Start-up" Position

The foreign worker may be destined to a ''start-up'' operation in Canada provided that the enterprise is established and can reasonably be expected to grow to a size sufficient to justify the foreign worker's anticipated employment activities at the level required to satisfy the criteria of this provision.

- The Canadian enterprise must be clearly established.

- The Canadian enterprise must not have been created merely to permit the transfer. *There must be employees or the prospects for active growth.*

(d) The Relationship Between the Member Nation and Canadian Enterprises

- The Canadian employer and foreign transferor business must be related either by way of parent, subsidiary or affiliate relationship.

The definition of ''affiliate'' includes common ownership of the transferor and transferee company by a third corporation or entity or group of companies. The Canadian operation may also be a branch of the transferor company.

5.4.4 DOCUMENTATION REQUIRED IN SUPPORT OF APPLICATION

- Proof of citizenship in a member nation listed in Appendix 5-A or proof of permanent residence in a member nation listed in Appendix 5-B.

- A letter from the foreign member nation enterprise that:

  - confirms the applicant has been employed continuously by the enterprise for at least one year immediately preceding the date of the application;

  - outlines the applicant's current position in an executive or managerial capacity, or one involving specialized knowledge. *The letter should stipulate the applicant's position, title, place in the enterprise and job description;*

  - confirms the applicant's citizenship in a member nation and residence in a member nation;

  - confirms that the applicant's specialized knowledge, if this is the basis of the application, is not available in Canada;

  - indicates the duration of the applicant's intended stay in Canada;

  - indicates the source and amount of the applicant's remuneration while in Canada; and

  - describes the relationship between the Canadian and the foreign member nation enterprise.

- Tangible proof of the relationship between the Canadian and foreign member nation enterprise.

- Evidence of the enterprise's employees and prior business record.

- Where the applicant is a specialist, and requires professional credentials to discharge her or his duties, evidence that the person has such credentials. (Photocopies of degree/diplomas and/or professional accreditation would constitute such evidence.)

- Where an enterprise has been established in Canada, the above-noted letter may be prepared and signed by an executive of the Canadian enterprise.

5.4.5 THE APPLICATION PROCESS

(a) Where to Apply

- Applications made pursuant to each category of the intra-company transferee provisions, may be submitted at the port of entry if the foreign worker does not need a visa to travel to Canada.

- If the applicant requires a visa to travel to Canada, the application must be submitted to a visa office abroad.

(b) Duration and Extensions

- The maximum period for issuance of the first employment authorization under the intra-company transferee category is one year.

- Up to two subsequent extensions may be obtained for a total stay of no more than three years. However, for executives and managers, immigration officials have a discretionary power to extend pursuant to section 20(5)(e)(i) of the *Regulations* if doing so would be in the best interest of Canada. Moreover, it may be possible to shift to another category in order to extend status in Canada if circumstances permit.

5.4.6 COMPARISON WITH NAFTA (CHAPTER 4) AND CODE E15 (CHAPTER 6)

Pursuant to the Code E15 job validation exemption, Canadian immigration policy already provides for the entry of intra-corporate transferees (only senior executives and managers, not lower level employees who merely possess specialized knowledge). The policy is derived from section 20(5)(e) of the *Regulations*. Moreover, under the NAFTA, similar transfer provisions exist. The NAFTA provisions apply to senior executives, senior managers and employees possessing certain types of specialized knowledge, who are United States and Mexican citizens being transferred to Canada. There are, however, distinct differences in the eligibility criteria:

- Pursuant to the GATS, the Canadian enterprise must be in a service sector specifically enumerated by the GATS. *The NAFTA and Code E15 job validation exemption have no such requirements.*

- The GATS requires that the applicant work for the employer outside of Canada for at least one year immediately preceding the application. *The NAFTA requires one year in the previous three years and the Code E15 job validation exemption has no stated minimum period.*

- In the GATS, there is a cap of three years imposed on the total duration of employment. *The NAFTA time cap is seven years for executives and managers, and five years for those persons with specialized knowledge, while the Code E15 job validation exemption may be extended beyond the five years stated in the policy guidelines in circumstances considered appropriate by the visa or immigration officer.*

5.5 PROFESSIONALS (ENTRY UNDER SECTION 20(5)(b)(i) OF THE *REGULATIONS*)

5.5.1 DEFINITION OF A PROFESSIONAL

A "professional" is a person who seeks to engage in an activity at a professional level in a profession set out in Appendix 5-D of this chapter.

- The activities to be performed by the applicant must be part of a services contract obtained by an enterprise in another member nation.

The list of eligible professions presently includes Engineers, Agrologists, Architects, Forestry Professionals, Geomatic Professionals and Land Surveyors. It will be expanded to include Legal Consultants, Urban Planners and Computer Specialists in June of 1996.

- Look to the applicant's job title and duties to determine if they are contemplated in Appendix 5-D.

5.5.2 QUALIFICATIONS AND REQUIREMENTS

(a) The Service Contract

- The service performed by the foreign professional must be related to a signed contract between the Canadian service consumer and the member nation service provider listed in Appendix 5-A.

- The contract cannot be between a service consumer and a foreign personnel placement agency or management consultant. The contract can provide for the payment of remuneration by the foreign service provider or the service consumer.

- The contract may be between a foreign service provider in a member nation or a Canadian-based company established by the service provider to sell its services in Canada.

(b) The Active Business

- The service provider must be engaged in business activity and have been established for a reasonable time. *A service provider that is merely a shell company or business entity will not qualify.*

(c) Professional Qualifications

- The applicant must possess the necessary academic credentials and professional qualifications which have been duly recognized, where appropriate, by the professional association in Canada.

- With respect to occupations for which licensing is not required, the issuance of the employment authorization can only be granted upon presentation of documentation from the appropriate professional association indicating that foreign academic credentials and professional qualifications are recognized. Unlike GATS intra-corporate transferees who possess specialized knowledge, GATS professionals, must obtain the necessary accreditation prior to entering Canada.

5.5.3 DOCUMENTATION REQUIRED IN SUPPORT OF APPLICATION

- Provide the following in support of the application:

  ○ photocopy of the signed contract between the foreign service provider and the Canadian service customer;

  ○ documentation evidencing the profession for which entry is sought;

  ○ documentation evidencing the province of destination;

  ○ documentation detailing the position (*for example, job description, duration of employment and remuneration arrangements*);

  ○ evidence that the applicant has professional qualifications or alternative credentials required to discharge their anticipated employment responsibilities; and

  ○ where required, a temporary or permanent licence issued by the appropriate provincial government.

5.5.4 THE APPLICATION PROCESS

(a) Where to Apply

- Employment authorizations based on the GATS professional category may be issued at the port of entry if a visitor visa is not required. Otherwise they must be obtained through a visa office abroad.

(b) Duration and Extension

- GATS professional-based employment authorizations cannot be issued for a period in excess of *three* months and cannot be renewed or extended thereafter.

In contrast, NAFTA professionals may obtain extensions to their employment authorizations provided that they continue to meet the requirements of the NAFTA.

5.6 CONCLUSION

The GATS does not meaningfully expand the restrictions to access of business persons and foreign workers to Canada generally found in the NAFTA or in the *Act* and *Regulations*.

The GATS provisions relating to the entry of business visitors are, in almost all cases, more restrictive than the provisions contained in the *Regulations*.

The intra-company transferee provisions are also restrictive as they relate to senior executives and senior managers. The provisions of the NAFTA and the *Regulations* are more generous. The GATS is, however, useful in obtaining admission for intra-company transferees who possess the required specialized knowledge but who do not qualify under the NAFTA.

The GATS professional category is not of any significant benefit in obtaining access to the Canadian labour market. Only six professions have been approved and included in Appendix 5-D, of which Engineers and Architects are occupations which are frequently used by foreign service providers. The inclusion in June of 1996 of Foreign Legal Consultants, Urban Planners and Computer Specialists will expand its applicability only marginally.

The NAFTA's provisions for professional employment in Canada are considerably more generous in terms of the number of occupations listed, as well as to periods of initial entry and subsequent extensions thereto. Further, the NAFTA does not present licensing as a prerequisite to the approval of the foreign worker's application. Clearly the NAFTA is truly designed to facilitate the movement of temporary foreign workers to Canada and should be resorted to whenever a United States or Mexican citizen is seeking an employment authorization as a professional.

Appendix 5-A

List of Member Nations

Angola
Antigua & Barbuda
Argentina
Australia
Austria
Bahrain
Bangladesh
Barbados
Belgium
Belize
Benin
Bolivia
Botswana
Brazil
Brunei
Burkina Faso
Burundi
Cameroon
Canada
Central African Republic
Chad
Chile
Colombia
Congo
Costa Rica
Cote d'Ivoire
Cuba
Cyprus
Czech Republic
Denmark
Dominica
Dominican Republic
Egypt
El Salvador
Fiji
Finland
France
Gabon
Gambia
Germany
Ghana

Grenada
Greece
Guatemala
Guinea-Bissau
Guyana
Haiti
Honduras
Hong Kong
Hungary
Iceland
India
Indonesia
Ireland
Israel
Italy
Jamaica
Japan
Kenya
Korea
Kuwait
Lesotho
Liechtenstein
Luxembourg
Macau
Madagascar
Malawi
Malaysia
Maldives
Mali
Malta
Mauritania
Mauritius
Mexico
Morocco
Mozambique
Myanmar
Namibia
Netherlands
New Zealand
Nicaragua
Niger

Nigeria
Norway
Pakistan
Paraguay
Peru
Philippines
Poland
Portugal
Qatar
Romania
Rwanda
Saint Lucia
St. Kitts & Nevis
St. Vincent & Grenada
Senegal
Sierra Leone
Singapore
Slovak Republic
Republic of South Africa
Spain
Sri Lanka
Suriname
Swaziland
Sweden
Switzerland
Tanzania
Thailand
Togo
Trinidad & Tobago
Tunisia
Turkey
Uganda
United Arab Emirates
United Kingdom
Uruguay
United States of America
Venezuela
Yugoslavia
Zaire
Zambia
Zimbabwe

Appendix 5-B

List of Member Nations Which Accord the Same Rights to Their Permanent Residents as to Their Citizens

No countries have notified to date.

Appendix 5-C

List of Service Sectors in Which Canada Has Made Commitments With Respect to Temporary Entry

Sectors covered

1. BUSINESS SERVICES
2. COMMUNICATION SERVICES
3. CONSTRUCTION SERVICES
4. DISTRIBUTION SERVICES
6. ENVIRONMENTAL SERVICE
7. FINANCIAL SERVICES
9. TOURISM AND TRAVEL RELATED SERVICES
11. TRANSPORT SERVICES

(Note: numbering is not sequential because Canada did not make commitments to sector numbers 5, 8 and 10.)

1. BUSINESS SERVICES

   A. Professional Services:
       — Foreign legal consultants
       — Accounting, auditing and bookkeeping services
       — Taxation services (excluding legal services)
       — Architectural services
       — Engineering services
       — Integrated engineering services
       — Urban planning and landscape architectural services
   B. Computer and Related Services:
       — Consultancy services related to the installation of computer hardware
       — Software implementation services, including systems and software consulting services, systems analysis, design, programming and maintenance services, excluding those listed under Financial Services
       — Data processing services, including processing, tabulation and facilities management services, excluding Communication Services (2C below) and Financial Services (7B below)
       — Data base services, excluding those listed under Financial Services
       — Maintenance and repair services of office machinery and equipment including computers
       — Other computer services
   C. Research and Development Services
       — Research and experimental development services on social sciences and humanities, including law and economics (excluding linguistics and language)
   D. Real Estate Services

139

— Real estate services involving own or leased property
— Real estate service on a fee or contract basis
E. Rental/Leasing Services without Operators
— Leasing or rental services concerning machinery and equipment without operator, including computers
— Leasing or rental services concerning personal and household goods (excluding the rental of pre-recorded records, sound cassettes, CDs and rental services concerning video tapes)
F. Other Business Services
— Market research and public opinion polling services
— Management consulting services
- General management consulting services
- Financial management consulting services
- Marketing management consulting services
- Human resources management consulting services
- Production management consulting services
- Public relations services
- Other management consulting services, including agrology, agronomy, farm management and related consulting services
— Services related to management consulting
— Technical testing and analysis services including quality control and inspection
— Rental of agricultural equipment with operator
— Services incidental to forestry and logging, including forest management
— Services incidental to mining, including drilling and field services and rental equipment with operator
- Site preparation for mining
— Tool refining services – oil and basic metals
— Placement and supply services of personnel
— Investigation and security services
— Related scientific and technical consulting services
— Geological, geophysical and other scientific prospecting services, including those related to mining
- Subsurface surveying services
- Surface surveying services
- Map making services
— Repair services of personal and household goods
- Repair services incidental to metal products, machinery and equipment including computers and communications equipment on a fee for contract basis
— Building-cleaning services
— Packaging services
— Other business services, including
- Credit reporting services
- Collection agency services
- Telephone answering services
- Duplicating services
- Translation and interpretation services
- Mailing list compilation and mailing services
- Specialty design services
- Patent services

2. COMMUNICATION SERVICES

A. Courier Services
   — Commercial courier services, including by public transport of self-owned transport

B. Telecommunication Services
   — Enhanced or value-added services, for the supply of which the underlying telecommunications transport facilities are leased from providers of public telecommunication transport networks; these include:
   - Electronic mail
   - Voice mail
   - On-line information and database retrieval
   - Electronic data interchange (EDI)
   - Enhanced/value-added facsimile services, including store and forward, store and retrieve
   - Code and protocol conversion
   - On-line information and/or data processing (including transaction processing)

3. CONSTRUCTION SERVICES

A. Commission Agents' Services
   — Commission agents services (excluding sales on a fee or contract basis of food products, beverages and tobacco and sales on a fee or contract basis of pharmaceutical and medical goods)
B. Wholesale Trade Services
   — Wholesale trade services (excepting agriculture and live animals; fisheries products; alcoholic beverages; musical scores, audio and video recording; and books, magazines, newspapers, journals, periodicals and other printed matter; and pharmaceutical and medical goods, and surgical and orthopaedic instruments and devices)
C. Retailing Services
   — Food retailing services (excluding liquor, wine and beer sales)
   — Non-food retailing services (excluding music scores, audio and video records and tapes; books, magazines, newspapers and periodicals; and pharmaceutical, medical and orthopaedic goods and printed music)
   — Sale of motor vehicles including automobiles and other road vehicles
   — Sale of parts and accessories of motor vehicles
   — Sales of motorcycles and snowmobiles and of related parts and accessories
D. Franchising
   — Franchising related to non-financial intangible assets
E. Other
   — Retail sales of motor fuel

4. ENVIRONMENTAL SERVICES

A. Sewage Services
B. Refuse Disposal Services
C. Sanitation and Similar Services
D. Other

— Cleaning services of exhaust gases
— Noise abatement services
— Nature and landscape protection services
— Other environmental services n.e.c.

5. FINANCIAL SERVICES

    A.   Insurance and Insurance-Related Services
          — Life, accident and health insurance services
          — Non-life insurance services (except deposit insurance and similar compensation schemes
          — Reinsurance and retrocession
          — Services auxiliary to insurance (including broking and agency services)
    B.   Banking and Other Financial Services (excluding insurance)
          — Acceptance of deposits and other repayable funds from the public
          — Lending of all types, including, inter alia, consumer credit, mortgage credit, factoring and financing of commercial transactions
          — Financial leasing
          — All payment and money transmission services
          — Guarantees and commitments
          — Trading for own account or for account of customers, whether on an exchange, in an over-the-counter market or otherwise, the following:
             • money market instruments (cheques, bills, certificates of deposit, etc.)
             • foreign exchange
             • derivative products including but not limited to, futures and options
             • exchange rate and interest rate instruments, including products such as swaps, forward rate agreements, etc.
             • transferable securities
             • other negotiable instruments and financial assets, including bullion
          — Participation in issues of all kinds of securities, including underwriting and placement as agent (whether publicly or privately) and provision of service related to such issues
          — Money broking
          — Asset management, such as cash or portfolio management, all forms of collective investment management, pension fund management, custodial depository and trust services
          — Settlement and clearing services for financial assets, including securities, derivative products, and other negotiable instruments
          — Advisory and other auxiliary financial services on activities including credit reference and analysis, investment and portfolio research and advice, advice on acquisitions and on corporate restructuring and strategy
          — Provision and transfer of financial information, and financial data processing and related software by providers of other financial services

6. TOURISM AND TRAVEL RELATED SERVICES

    A.   Hotels and Restaurants (including catering)

— Hotel and other lodging services
— Food and beverage serving services
B.   Travel Agencies and Tour Operators Services
— Travel agency and tour operator services

7. TRANSPORT SERVICES

A.   Maritime Transport Services
C.   Air Transport Services
— Maintenance and repair of aircraft and aircraft engines
— Computer reservations systems
E.   Rail Transport Services
— Railway passenger and Freight transport
— Maintenance and repair of rail transport equipment
F.   Road Transport Services
— Passenger transportation
  • Interurban scheduled bus passenger transportation
  • Taxis
  • Rental services of cars with drivers
  • Nonscheduled motor buses, chartered buses and tour and sight-seeing buses
— Freight transportation
  • Highway freight transportation
— Rental of commercial vehicle with operator
  • Rental services of commercial road vehicles with operators
  • Maintenance of road transport equipment
  • Maintenance and repair services of motor vehicles
  • Maintenance and repair services of motorcycles and snowmobiles
  • Repair services n.e.c. of motor vehicles, trailer, semi-trailers on a fee or contract basis
H.   Services Auxiliary to All Modes of Transport Other than Maritime Auxiliary Services
— Container handling services
  • Other cargo handling services
— Storage and warehouse services
— Freight transport agency services
— Other supporting and auxiliary transport services, including freight forwarding
  • Storage and warehousing services
  • Customs clearance services (as defined)
  • Container station and depot services (as defined)
  • Maritime agency services
  • Maritime freight forwarding services (as defined)

Appendix 5-D

List of Professional Occupations, Together With Minimum Educational Requirements/Alternative Credentials and Other [Licensing] Requirements

Occupation	Minimum Educational Requirements/Alternative Credentials	Other Requirement
Engineers	Baccalaureate degree*	Provincial licence**
Agrologists	Baccalaureate degrees in agriculture or related science plus four years of related experience	Licensing is required in New Brunswick, Alberta and Quebec. Temporary licensing is required in British Columbia.
Architects	Baccalaureate degree in architecture	Provincial licence and certificate required to practise.
Forestry Professionals	Baccalaureate degree in forestry management or forestry engineering, or a provincial licence	Licensing as a forester or forestry engineer is required in Alberta, British Columbia and Quebec.
Geomatics Professionals***	Baccalaureate degree in surveying, geography or environmental science plus three years related experience	
Land Surveyors	Baccalaureate degree	Provincial licence.

    * Baccalaureate degree means a degree from an accredited academic institution in Canada or equivalent
   ** Provincial licence means any document issued by a provincial government, or under its authority, which permits a person to engage in a regulated activity or profession
 *** Geomatics Professional must be working in aerial surveying or aerial photography.

6

EMPLOYMENT AUTHORIZATIONS

6.1 INTRODUCTION

- In the event that entry cannot be obtained under one of the exemptions to the requirement to obtain an employment authorization, such as business visitor status as defined in the North American Free Trade Agreement ("NAFTA") or the General Agreement on Trade in Services ("GATS"), counsel should determine whether the applicant qualifies for an employment authorization.

6.2 DEFINITION OF "EMPLOYMENT"

"Employment" means "any activity for which a person receives or might reasonably be expected to receive valuable consideration". See section 2 of the *Immigration Act (Act)*. Any activities which are compensatory if performed by an arm's length party constitute employment. See *Georgas v. Canada (Min. of Employment and Immigration)*, [1979] F.C. 349 (Fed. C.A.).

The basic purpose of the *Act*, in relation to the authorization of foreign employment, is to ensure that work opportunities are not denied to Canadian citizens or permanent residents as a result of the entry of foreign workers to Canada.

- When deciding whether a visitor requires an employment authorization, three factors are considered by immigration officers:

  ○ cash remuneration: whether the visitor (or any third party on the visitor's behalf) will receive cash remuneration for the activity;

  ○ goods or services: whether the visitor will receive goods or services as remuneration (*for example, room and board*); and

○ valuable consideration: whether valuable consideration might reasonably be expected to be received from the visitor's activities, even if none has been promised to the foreign worker.

Immigration officers will require foreign relatives to obtain employment authorizations in order to assist family members in Canada where such assistance is of a regular and ongoing nature. If a foreign relative enters Canada to assist a family member in a crisis situation for a temporary period of time, an employment authorization may not be required.

6.3 EMPLOYMENT AUTHORIZATIONS— GENERAL INFORMATION

Persons who do not qualify as visitors under the *Immigration Regulations* (*Regulations*), the NAFTA or the GATS are required to apply for a Foreign Worker Record (also known as a job validation or employment validation and formerly known as a Confirmation of Offer of Employment, 5056 or 2151) prior to applying for an employment authorization unless they qualify under one or more of the various of the categories listed in this section or in the non-business visitor provisions of the NAFTA or the GATS. Persons who do not qualify under one of these categories, will be required to obtain a Foreign Worker Record prior to applying for an employment authorization (see Chapter 7). Accordingly, the categories listed in the *Immigration Manual* are those which are applicable to citizens of all nations, and which are described in this chapter, are called "validation exempt categories". These categories have been established by immigration policy and are set out in Chapter 15 of the *Immigration Manual*.

Be aware that many of these categories are open to the subjective interpretation of the immigration officer evaluating the application. The submission of a legal memorandum with the application for temporary entry to Canada will assist the subjective determination of an immigration officer. Immigration officials may differ quite substantially in relation to their interpretation of the applicability of the categories outlined in the succeeding sections of this chapter. Nonetheless, the various categories under this chapter provide counsel with substantial opportunities to argue for a client's temporary entry to Canada.

The validation exemptions set out below are referred to in a general manner in the *Regulations* and the general categories appearing in the *Regulations* are further subdivided in Chapter 15 of the *Immigration Manual* and are set out below.

6.3.1 VALIDATION EXEMPTIONS UNDER SECTION 20(5)(e)(i)

Section 20(5)(e)(i) of the *Regulations* states as follows:

> . . . a person in respect of paragraph 1(a) should not, in the opinion of the immigration officer, be applied for the reason that
>
> (i) his employment will create or maintain significant employment, benefits or opportunities for Canadian citizens or permanent residents, . . .

This section of the *Regulations* creates a wide category for foreign workers whose employment in Canada is anticipated to create significant employment, benefits or opportunities for Canadians. Policymakers have created specific exemption codes under this general exemption. These specific exemptions are detailed in a series of "codes" further explained below.

(a) Self-employed Persons — Code E01

This category applies to individuals wishing to enter Canada for purposes of becoming self-employed in various capacities.

- The applicant would be entering Canada for purposes of establishing a business for which Canadian citizens and permanent residents would be recruited or trained. *Self-employed applicants are admitted to Canada because it is anticipated that they will create and maintain significant employment, benefits or opportunities for Canadian citizens and permanent residents (i.e., hiring secretarial staff, making orders to Canadian suppliers, contracting with Canadian companies, etc.).*

- Because of their contribution to the economy of Canada, persons applying under this category are not required to obtain a validation prior to applying for an employment authorization.

- Persons seeking entry into Canada under this exemption are generally wealthy business persons from other countries who have a proven record of success.

147

- Investment potential without business experience may be sufficient in order to qualify under this category.

  Be aware that certain immigration officers are of the view that employment authorizations issued under this exemption should be difficult to extend on the theory that the exemption was designed for people who were coming to Canada to set up a business and then leave the business in the hands of the Canadians who were recruited or trained for that business. This interpretation is no longer supported by the text of the Immigration Manual.

Documentary Requirements:

- The applicant should provide substantial evidence of financial ability to make an investment in Canada or establish a business for which Canadian citizens or permanent residents will be recruited or trained. *It may be sufficient to show financial statements or bank records from the applicant's foreign company as these could indicate previous business success.*

- Regardless of the amount invested, self-employed applicants are required to provide detailed information concerning their anticipated business activities in Canada as well as the manner and number of Canadian citizens and permanent residents to be recruited or trained.

  Immigration officers may also request additional financial information including information about the financial circumstances of the applicant and may request a transfer of a portion of the anticipated investment to a Canadian banking institution, in the event that the applicant does not have a foreign company, the financial statements do not indicate sufficient Canadian funds or the financial statements or taxation returns of the applicant are unreliable.

- The applicant should be advised to submit a business proposal particularizing the contemplated activities in Canada including the name, location, nature and extent of the business to be established in Canada.

- Entry under this category must be clearly substantiated and the applicant should be advised to make a visit to Canada to solidify and concretize her or his plans prior to applying for a self-employed temporary employment authorization.

  Depending on the proposed business, however, substantial assets may not necessarily be required, particularly if the applicant has been demonstrably successful in countries with a similar economic climate to Canada which resulted in the employment of local workers or involved similar benefits to the local economy.

- The lower the amount that the applicant intends to invest or has invested in Canada under this category, the higher the burden of proof will be to demonstrate that significant employment, benefits or opportunities to Canadian citizens and permanent residents, will be created through the entry of the foreign worker.

(b) Entrepreneurial Applicants/Pre-Landing Entry— Code E03

This validation exempt category applies to persons who are entrepreneurial immigrants and who are allowed to enter Canada to establish a business leading to eventual landing. Persons who would qualify under this category are persons who would likely qualify as entrepreneurs, in the event that they applied for permanent residence, or are already permanent residence applicants under the entrepreneur category, whose applications for permanent residence have not been completed and require immediate entry in order to commence their business activities in Canada.

- An entrepreneur applicant wishing to enter Canada temporarily may submit her or his application for temporary entry to Canada prior to or during the processing of the application for permanent residence in Canada.

  Immigration officers processing applications for permanent residence are authorized to allow applicants or pro-

149

*spective applicants temporary entry to Canada by provid-
ing them with a Minister's Permit.*

- The applicant should be advised that a more expeditious
  manner of ensuring a relatively speedy entry to Canada is
  to apply for temporary employment authorizations under
  the self-employed (Code E01) category rather than the entrepreneur (Code E03) category, because the latter generally requires the applicant to await her or his interview
  at a processing post prior to a determination being made
  in relation to their temporary entry to Canada.

- The applicant should be cautioned to ensure that the application for an employment authorization be consistent
  with the intended business activities set out in the application for permanent residence in the event that she or he
  has already made application for permanent residence in
  Canada.

(c) Self-employed Person/Non-employment Related Benefits—Code E05

This exemption relates to self-employed persons who seek to enter Canada temporarily and where their admission will result in significant benefits or opportunities
to Canada other than direct employment to Canadian citizens or permanent residents.

- *Inter alia*, this exemption applies to expert witnesses who
  enter Canada for purposes of conducting studies, surveys,
  analysis which may be ultimately used in testimony at administrative tribunals, boards or courts. *The entry of these
  expert witnesses ensures that Canadians receive expert
  assistance in administrative or court proceedings so as to
  ensure fairness and impartiality regardless of the availability of Canadian expertise.*

- Prior to applying under this category as an expert witness,
  counsel should ensure that the client does not qualify under
  section 19(1)(p) of the *Regulations* ". . . as an expert witness for the sole purpose of testifying at proceedings before a regulatory board or tribunal or a court." *The section*

19(1)(p) exemption to the requirement to obtain an employment authorization only applies to witnesses who enter for the purpose of testifying.

In addition, this exemption has, for example, been used to gain temporary admission for actors, directors and other entertainment-related applicants, as well as for self-employed artists and businesspeople whose Canadian business activities will result in significant artistic, cultural or economic benefits to Canada. Accordingly, this exemption has potentially far-reaching applications.

Documentary Requirements:

- An expert witness making an application for an employment authorization under this category is required to provide documentary evidence indicating her or his expertise in the relevant area.

- The applicant must also provide documentation demonstrating that she or he is required to conduct a study, survey or analysis which would ultimately be used as testimony in proceedings before a regulatory body, tribunal or court.

- The applicant should provide immigration officers with a curriculum vitae as well as academic qualifications or letters of reference indicating expertise in a certain subject matter which will be addressed by the study, survey or analysis which would ultimately be used as testimony and which she or he is required to perform while in Canada.

- Other types of self-employed applicants are often required to provide copies of previous income tax returns in which they have declared income from self-employment.

(d) Foreign Workers Installing/Servicing/Repairing Specialized Equipment Exemption—Code E10

This particular exemption relates to four kinds of activities, all of which involve specialized equipment.

(i) Supervision of Installation of Special Machinery Purchased or Leased Outside Canada

Foreign workers may enter Canada to supervise the installation of specialized machinery purchased or leased outside Canada or, alternatively, to supervise the dismantling of equipment or machinery purchased in Canada for relocation outside Canada.

- This subcategory only applies to a supervisor and not to a foreign worker who is actually involved in the installation.

- The duties of the person seeking entry to Canada must be consistent with the duties of a supervisor.

- One supervisor is expected to supervise five to ten installers or other workers.

(ii) Foreign Workers Repairing or Servicing

- A foreign worker repairing or servicing specialized equipment purchased or leased outside of Canada may enter Canada in a non-supervisory capacity to repair or service specialized equipment in the event that such services are required as part of the original or extended sales agreement, lease agreement, warranty or service contract.

- The entry of the foreign worker is conditional on services performed being part of the original or extended sales agreement, lease agreement, warranty or service contract.

  Any service agreements which are not part of the original sales agreement, lease agreement, warranty or service contract or an extension thereto, will not fall within the ambit of this section.

- In the case of an extension of the original sales or lease agreement, the extension ought to be signed or agreed to by the same parties who signed the original sales or lease agreement. Otherwise, service contracts negotiated with third parties are not covered by the exemption and a validated offer of employment would be required.

(iii) Foreign Workers Providing Familiarization of Services

This subcategory allows the foreign worker to enter Canada to provide familiarization of services to prospective users or maintenance staff after the installation of specialized equipment which has been purchased or leased outside of Canada has been completed.

- There is no requirement that the installation of the specialized equipment be supervised by the foreign worker under subcategory 1 of Code E10.

- The foreign worker seeking entry to provide familiarization services must provide a letter from the foreign company indicating the reason for the requirement of familiarization with the equipment for prospective users or maintenance staff at the Canadian company.

- The applicant should be advised to provide the immigration officer with a copy of the sales or lease agreement.

(iv) Members of Crews of Specialized Railroad Track Maintenance Trains Entering Canada Under Contract to a Canadian Railway for Rail Grinding, Ballast Cleaning or Rail Inspecting

This subcategory specifically applies to members of crews of specialized railroad track maintenance trains (Sperry Cars).

- The *Immigration Manual* stipulates that such crews should come to Canada under a contract and a copy of the contract should be made available to immigration officers for their review.

- The duties to be performed by such crews may be supervisory or worker related.

(e) Intra-Corporate Transfer Category—Code E15

Be aware that this intra-corporate transfer category is less restrictive than the intra-corporate transfer categories under the NAFTA and the GATS relating to senior executives and managers. Whenever possible, intra-company transferees should be brought under this category.

- Persons qualifying under this category are employed by a branch, subsidiary or parent of the Canadian company, located outside of Canada.

- Applicants must be employed in a senior managerial or senior executive capacity at the Canadian company.

- Intra-company transfers must be of a temporary nature *(i.e., to oversee operations, to establish the company, etc.).*

- The company in Canada must be of a permanent and continuing nature and not a vehicle by which the intra-corporate transferee may gain access to Canada.

- Intra-corporate transfer status will not be given to persons in low managerial positions or in a mere supervisory capacity.

- Persons seeking entry to Canada must be acting in a senior executive or managerial capacity in the foreign-related company prior to the transfer to the Canadian branch, subsidiary or parent corporation. *The applicant is not required, by policy, to be acting in a senior executive or managerial capacity for a minimum period of time prior to entering Canada. However, the applicant's position at the foreign-related company must be, unambiguously, senior executive or managerial and the position to which the transferee will be transferred to Canada must likewise be senior executive or managerial. Middle management or junior management positions will not qualify for consideration under the intra-corporate transfer category. Persons operating in a managerial capacity at construction or engineering sights or projects will not be allowed to enter under the intra-corporate transfer category.*

154

An employment authorization issued under this category may be valid for an initial period of a maximum of three years. Subsequent extensions, of one year in duration, may be obtained. General policy provides that the total stay should not exceed five years. This policy, however, can rather easily be overcome in appropriate circumstances.

Documentary Requirements:

- Generally, it is sufficient to obtain a letter from the Canadian branch, subsidiary or parent company inviting the senior executive/manager and specifying the following:

  ○ The legal relationship between the Canadian and foreign entities.

  ○ That the applicant has been employed at the foreign-related branch subsidiary or parent company located outside of Canada in a senior executive or managerial category.

  ○ The duties of the senior executive/manager at the branch, subsidiary or parent company located outside of Canada.

  ○ A statement that the applicant is being transferred to the branch, subsidiary or parent of the company located outside of Canada in a senior executive or managerial capacity.

  ○ The duties or responsibilities of the applicant once she or he arrives in Canada.

  ○ The period of time that the senior executive/manager will be required in Canada.

  ○ Information and background relating to the company located outside of Canada as well as the business activities of the branch, subsidiary or parent in Canada indicating that the company in Canada is a permanent and continuing company.

◦ Information about the applicant's credentials, background and qualifications in order to demonstrate that she or he is qualified to assume the duties required by the Canadian company;

- Immigration and visa officers may require additional evidence indicating that the Canadian company is a legitimate entity, particularly if the senior executive/manager is entering Canada for the purpose of establishing the company.

- Documentary evidence such as financial statements, corporate records, supplier or distribution agreements, consulting agreements, leases, client lists and any other evidence indicative of the company's operations in Canada will facilitate the application process considerably. *Detailed documentation will not normally be necessary in the case of established companies.*

- In the event that the Canadian company was recently incorporated and very little business has been commenced in Canada to date, rather than concentrating on the Canadian subsidiary, the applicant should provide substantive information relating to the foreign parent company which would indirectly demonstrate the potential of the Canadian subsidiary.

   ◦ Such information would include financial statements and/ or forecasts or projections, as well as background information indicating that the foreign company has had a background of success and stability.

   Counsel may also want to furnish further documentation relating to the Canadian company, particularly if the Canadian company is a subsidiary of the foreign parent corporation.

- The senior executive/manager should provide a copy of the employment contract evidencing her or his senior role in the company and showing a salary that is representative of the senior position.

- Some immigration and visa officers will request a letter from the foreign company indicating that its employee shall be transferred to the Canadian subsidiary.

- In order to encourage the expeditious processing of an intra-company transfer application, counsel should include all the documentation to be submitted to the processing post with the original application.

(f) Significant Benefit for Canada — Code E19

This category was also "carved out" of section 20(5)(e)(i) of the *Regulations* for applicants who do not fall squarely within the categories specified earlier in this chapter (i.e., Codes EO1, EO5, E10 and E15) as well as the other categories set out in Chapter 15 of the *Immigration Manual*.

Immigration or visa officers will use this category where the admission of persons seeking entry to Canada will create or maintain significant benefits or opportunities for Canadians not related to employment. Immigration officers will consider whether the benefits and opportunities offered to Canadian citizens or permanent residents by the applicants' admission to Canada are "significant" in nature. Activities falling within the policy guidelines of this section are set out below but are not exhaustive.

- American media crews on tourism or promotional tours may be exempt from employment validation if:

  ○ they are in possession of a letter of invitation extended by Canadian federal/provincial or territorial governments;

  ○ the total crew size does not exceed three persons, including writers, film crews and broadcast journalists and technicians; and

  ○ their stay does not exceed two weeks.

- Non-North American media crews will fall within the ambit of this exemption from the requirement to obtain an employment validation, if:

  ○ the total crew size does not exceed three people;

157

   ○ the length of stay does not exceed six weeks; and

   ○ the final product must be available for distribution and
     viewing by non-North American audiences and markets.

 • Media crews not meeting conditions of the above two subcategories will be validation exempt if they do not meet
   any of the following conditions:

   ○ the crew size exceeds three persons;

   ○ the crew wishes to remain in Canada for more than two
     weeks (American crews) or more than six weeks (non-
     American crews);

   ○ the invitation has been extended by a party other than
     a Canadian federal, provincial or territorial government;
     or

   ○ material is being produced for distribution in, or viewing
     by, North American markets and audiences (non-Amer-
     ican crews).

The *Immigration Manual* clarifies that this category is not restricted to the above
activities and the immigration or visa officer reviewing an application under this
general category is required to assess each application on the merits and is allowed
to exercise full discretion in making a determination on whether a particular activity
would create or maintain a significant benefit or opportunity to Canadian citizens
and permanent residents.

Chapter 15.15(4)(f) of the *Immigration Manual* provides guidance to immigration
officers as follows:

> The realm of possibilities here is bound only by one's judgment and the emphasis
> should be on the term "significant" which appears in the *Regulations*.

Counsel should encourage immigration officers to exercise their wide discretion
under this section by providing them with creative and reasonable arguments.
However, the level of scrutiny in relation to this category is substantial and, depending on the immigration officer's seniority, may require approval by a second
(senior) visa officer.

(g) Student Employment Situations

There are three validation exemption codes under section 20(5)(e)(i) of the *Regulations* which apply to student employment situations involving students or their spouses who are in full-time school.

(i) Code E06

This code applies to full-time students at a post-secondary institution who obtain employment in campus by either the institution, faculty, student organization or private contractor providing services to the institution.

(ii) Code E07

This code applies to spouses of full-time post-secondary school students. The employment authorization will be provided to a spouse who is not a student for a period not exceeding the student authorization of the full-time student.

(iii) Code E08

This exemption is quite significant for students who have completed their post-secondary school education and who wish to obtain employment in Canada immediately after their academic program.

- The applicant must meet the following criteria in order to qualify for a validation exempt employment authorization under this category:

  - Successful completion of post-secondary school program.

  - Employment must commence within sixty days of release of final marks by the institution.

  - The employment must be consistent with the student's area of study.

  - The duration of employment must not exceed one year — no extensions are provided unless the person qualifies for a validated offer of employment.

159

○ The student is required to make application for an employment authorization while her or his student authorization is valid.

○ The employment may involve more than one employer provided that it does not extend beyond one year.

6.4 VALIDATION EXEMPTIONS UNDER REGULATION 20(5)(e)(ii)

This validation code is applied to persons seeking entry to Canada for the purpose of engaging in non-remunerative employment at Canadian religious and charitable organizations.

If entry is sought to perform work for a charitable organization, the organization must be recognized as charitable by Revenue Canada. Employment sought under this category must not involve remuneration (i.e., a salary) but may involve a stipend.

This chapter will not focus on this exemption as it does not generally apply to business immigrants.

6.5 VALIDATION EXEMPTION UNDER REGULATION 20(5)(e)(iii)

This exemption is probably one of the most under-utilized employment authorization categories notwithstanding the fact that it is based on the general principle of reciprocity. Persons qualifying under this section are applicants whose employment would result in reciprocal employment of Canadian citizens in other countries.

Various subcategories are listed under this exemption:

-Code E30 applies to foreign students.

-Code E35 applies to international student and young worker employment programs.

-Code E45 applies to graduate assistants, teaching assistants, research assistants.

-Code E50 applies to commuters to the United States of America.

-Code E95 applies to amateur athletes and amateur coaches.

6.5.1 CODE E99

Code E99 applies to reciprocal employment opportunities of Canadians abroad. Code E99 can be a useful tool in order to assist a foreign worker who would not otherwise qualify for a validation exempt category. It is rarely used by visa officers notwithstanding that many types of employment provide specific reciprocal employment opportunities for Canadians abroad.

Example:

A musician from England may be allowed to enter Canada on the basis that there is a reciprocal opportunity for a Canadian musician in England. Accordingly, any type of reciprocal employment should be sufficient to make a fairly persuasive argument that the foreign worker qualifies under this section.

This exemption has been used successfully to obtain employment authorizations for individuals destined for Canadian employers who have sent Canadians to work abroad, as well as for spouses of employment authorization holders where the employment authorization holder comes from a jurisdiction which allows spouses of temporary foreign workers to engage in employment.

Immigration officers often differ in their views of what is considered a "reciprocol" employment opportunity.

Documentary Requirements:

- Counsel should provide evidence in the form of documentation indicating the reciprocal employment opportunities provided to Canadians in the jurisdiction in question.

- A letter of invitation setting out the nature of the duties of the applicant in Canada, should the employment authorization be approved. Such duties must be consistent with the duties required for the reciprocal employment opportunity in the applicant's jurisdiction.

6.6 VALIDATION EXEMPTION UNDER SECTION 20(5)(d) OF THE *REGULATIONS*

This exemption relates to foreign worker employment involving research, educational or training programs that have been approved by the Minister. Various subcategories are mentioned under this category and it is suggested that the Minister's office be consulted in addition to the *Immigration Manual* in relation to these government-approved programs. Scientists who, although they have not been invited to Canada by a Canadian institution or company, but have been approved by the Ministry of Industry, Trade and Technology to conduct independent research in Canada, are included within the ambit of this section.

This exemption also allows the entry of students to Canada either through the sponsorship of the Canadian International Development Agency ("CIDA") or students whose employment is an "essential and integral" part of their studies in Canada.

Counsel should be aware that the application process under this category is often time consuming because this exemption involves a number of procedural requirements with various governmental organizations.

6.7 MAKING AN APPLICATION FOR AN EMPLOYMENT AUTHORIZATION

6.7.1 GENERAL PROCEDURAL STEPS

- Steps involved in obtaining an employment authorization:

  - The applicant must create or obtain an employment position in Canada.

  - The applicant must decide on the processing post where the application will be submitted.

  - The applicant must normally submit an application along with the requisite documentation.

  - The applicant may be required to attend an interview.

  - The applicant may be required to undergo medical examinations.

  - If applying at a post outside of Canada, the successful applicant will receive a "Letter of Authorization" which she or he will present to immigration officers at the port of entry.

  - Application at the port of entry entails the presentation of the required documentation to immigration officials and the possible examination of the applicant.

○ If successful, the applicant will be provided with an employment authorization at the port of entry.

6.7.2 THE APPLICATION PROCESS

- The process of making an application for a temporary employment authorization can be somewhat complex as there are various aspects of the processes to consider:

  ○ the category of application;

  ○ the processing post;

  ○ the documentation required;

  ○ the strategy depending on the applicant's qualifications and the timing of the application process.

(a) Where to Apply

- There are generally three options available to a person wishing to make an application for an employment authorization:

  1. processing post abroad *(i.e., a Canadian consulate, embassy, or high commission)*;

  2. inland processing post *(i.e., a local Canada immigration centre or case processing centre)*; and

  3. port of entry.

Be aware that not all of the options mentioned below are available to all applicants: Code E01 applicants are barred from making an application at a port of entry as the documentation generally submitted by such applicants is voluminous. Immigration officers at ports of entry do not have large periods of uninterrupted time in which to consider a time consuming application and are not equipped to process lengthy applications.

(i) Processing Post Abroad

Persons requiring visitor visas prior to entering Canada are required to apply for their visas and employment authorizations at a visa office abroad.

(ii) Port of Entry

Generally, persons applying for an employment authorization at the port of entry are visa exempt individuals. All applications for temporary status for such persons will be processed at a port of entry unless they are voluminous or require verification. For example, applications under the self-employed and entrepreneur categories generally should be made at a processing post abroad because these kinds of applications are somewhat complex and involve substantial documentation. Otherwise, all other applications for employment authorizations may be processed at the port of entry.

(iii) Inland

Certain individuals, such as people who entered Canada as business visitors under the NAFTA and immediate family members of individuals who hold employment authorizations, may apply for employment authorizations inland.

(b) Visa and Employment Applications

- In the event that the applicant requires a visa prior to making entry to Canada, the employment application must be accompanied by the usual cost recovery fee and possibly a fee for the visitor visa, particularly if a multiple-entry visa is required. *Visa offices are not consistent in the application of fees policy in this regard. However, a separate visa application form is usually not required.*

(c) Documentation

- The application package which is to be sent to the processing post or presented to the processing post in person should contain the following:

○ Application form (i.e., Application for Temporary Entry into Canada for processing posts abroad or the Application to Vary or Change Terms of Admission for processing posts within Canada). Sample copies of both application forms are attached as appendices 6-A and 6-B. No application forms are required at the port of entry.

○ Copy of or original (if visa required) passport of applicant.

○ Curriculum vitae of applicant.

○ Letter of invitation from Canadian employer which sets out:

1. the duties to be performed by applicant;

2. the salary;

3. the date of commencement; and

4. the date of termination of employment.

or if the applicant is a self-employed applicant:

1. documentary proof of the applicant's net worth; and

2. a business proposal.

• The immigration or visa officer may request additional information such as documentation which would indicate that the applicant will return to her or his country of residence or that the company employing the individual is legitimate and that the job offer is valid.

(d) Medical Requirements

• Foreign workers will be required to undergo medical examinations prior to the approval of an employment authorization if they come from certain geographical areas (set out in Chapter 2, Appendix 2-D) or if they fall within the following categories:

○ workers in the health services field

○ teachers teaching children under the age of 18

○ live-in caregivers

○ workers who give in-home care to children, the elderly and the disabled

○ day nursery employees

○ camp counsellors

○ agricultural workers

6.7.3 DURATION OF EMPLOYMENT AUTHORIZATION

Employment authorizations may be issued for an initial period of up to three years, although one year is most common. Policy dictates that visa or immigration officers should normally limit the total period of validity of the employment authorization to five years, absent extraordinary circumstances. Keep in mind, however, that the NAFTA and the GATS contain their own time limits. These time limits apply regardless of whether or not the temporary employment authorization is supported by a job validation.

- In the event that the temporary foreign worker requires a visa, the validity of the employment authorization should not exceed the validity of the visa.

- If passports or travel documents are required, the validity of the employment authorization should not exceed the validity of the passport or travel document.

Certain classes of temporary employment authorizations may only be provided for one year at a time. Although the categories do not relate to business immigration, they are significant in scope and a list of them is annexed as Appendix 6-C.

6.8 PROCESSING LETTERS OF AUTHORIZATION AT A PORT OF ENTRY

- Upon obtaining a Letter of Authorization indicating approval of an application for a temporary employment authorization by a processing post abroad, the applicant may appear at a port of entry and request an employment authorization. *Generally, the level of scrutiny at the port of entry relates to the person's identity as opposed to the substantive merits of the application for temporary entry to Canada.*

- Once the port of entry immigration officer is satisfied that she or he is in a position to issue an employment authorization, a computerized record which specifies the nature, duration and place of employment will be attached to the foreign worker's passport or travel document.

- Each foreign worker is issued an employment authorization which should list any family members or dependants accompanying the foreign worker to Canada. The accompanying dependants should be granted a visitor record stipulating the duration of their stay in Canada.

- The applicant should be advised that the employment authorization will be denied if her or his statement contradict the information contained in the computer file relating to her or his employment authorization, as set out by the visa officer at the processing post abroad.

6.8.1 TERMS AND CONDITIONS AND LIMIT ON DURATION

- Section 23(3) of the *Regulations* specifies the various terms and conditions which may be attached to the employment authorization of a foreign worker (these have been enumerated in Chapter 2). If terms or conditions are imposed, they will appear on the employment authorization.

- A foreign worker is required to comply with any terms or conditions imposed on her or his employment authorization (see section 18(2) of the *Regulations*). *Individuals in possession of an employment authorization should be advised to comply strictly with all terms and conditions specified in the authorization.*

6.8.2 PORT OF ENTRY IMMIGRATION OFFICERS

Immigration officers at ports of entry are responsible for determining whether a person is eligible for entry to Canada and may make a decision on the merits of the application in light of the qualifications of the applicant. Port-of-entry immigration officers may make determinations on most applications for temporary employment authorizations including employment which requires Canada Employment Centre approval and employment that is validation exempt.

If an employment authorization has been approved at a processing post outside of Canada, port-of-entry immigration officers are required to finalize the process by providing applicants with the actual employment authorization. Although they have power equal to that of visa officers, they should not second guess the visa officer and deny the employment authorization unless they suspect fraud or a material change in circumstances.

6.9 APPLYING FOR EXTENSIONS ON TEMPORARY WORK AUTHORIZATIONS

- Once in Canada, there are three ways of obtaining an extension to a temporary employment authorization (assuming an extension has already been obtained for the employment validation if required):

  1. processing post abroad (*technically, this is not an extension but rather a new application*);

  2. port of entry; and

  3. inland processing posts (*i.e., the Case Processing Centre in Vegreville and, where possible, local Canada immigration centres*).

- The general rule is that an extension should be obtained from an inland processing post.

- Counsel should note that because of considerable backlogs at inland processing posts it may be more expeditious to renew a client's status at a processing post abroad or at a port of entry.

- Extending status at a processing post abroad is a more certain route than at a port of entry given the fact that the former post will generally provide the applicant the opportunity to provide further information substantiating their application prior to rejecting the submission.

- If extending status at a port of entry, counsel should advise the applicant to decide whether the "on the spot" processing of their application to extend status outweighs the possible risk of being denied extension of status and, possibly, entry to Canada.

6.10 CHANGING FROM ONE TEMPORARY STATUS TO ANOTHER

Often, once a foreign worker arrives in Canada, they discover other employment opportunities. While it is possible to change employers after arrival in Canada, applications to vary the terms and conditions of entry will be heavily scrutinized.

- The new employment position must fall within one of the employment validation exempt categories listed in the *Regulations* or, alternatively, must qualify for an employment validation. Most employment authorizations and all job validations are job specific.

- Where a change in status is sought, counsel should ensure that the applicant's visitor or employment status in Canada does not lapse prior to making application for a change of status.

6.11 STRATEGY FOR APPLYING FOR TEMPORARY EMPLOYMENT AUTHORIZATIONS

- The strategy in obtaining temporary entry is to avoid the lengthy application procedures necessitated by applying for a Foreign Worker Record (or employment validation).

- Whenever possible, counsel should attempt to qualify their clients under visitor status, pursuant to the NAFTA and GATS visitor categories set out in Chapters 4 and 5 or under one of the categories explained in this chapter. Particular emphasis should be placed on the validation exempt category codes E19, E99, E01 and E15.

Attached, as Appendix 6-D, and as a guide to the reader, is an excerpt from the *Immigration Manual* which is entitled "Temporary Foreign Worker Processing Summary".

Appendix 6-A

1. Surname (Family name) Nom de famille	First Name Prénom	Middle name Autres prénoms

2. Present address – Adresse actuelle	3. Address in home country – Adresse dans le pays d'origine
	☐ Same as in question 2 or Préciser si elle diffère de celle donnée au 2

Telephone number – Numéro de téléphone ▶

4. Date of Birth – Date de naissance			5. Place of Birth – Lieu de naissance			6. Citizen of Citoyenneté
D-J	M	Y-A	City/Town – Ville/Village	Prov./State - Prov./État	Country – Pays	

7. Sex – Sexe ☐ Male Homme ☐ Female Femme

8. Present marital status – État civil ☐ Unmarried (never married) Célibataire ☐ Engaged Fiancé(e) ☐ Married Marié(e) ☐ Widowed Veuf (Veuve) ☐ Separated Séparé(e) ☐ Divorced Divorcé(e)

9. Personal details of family members who will accompany me to Canada
Renseignements sur les membres de ma famille qui m'accompagneront au Canada

	Family name Nom de famille	First and second names Prénoms	Date and place of birth Date et lieu de naissance	Relationship to me Lien de parenté	Citizenship Citoyenneté
a)					
b)					
c)					
d)					
e)					
f)					

10. Passport details for myself and for persons listed in question 9
Précisions portées sur le passeport – Visiteur et personnes mentionnées au 9

	First name Prénom	Passport number N° du passeport	Country of issue Pays de délivrance	Date of issue Date de délivrance	Date of expiry Date d'expiration
	Applicant Requérant				
a)					
b)					
c)					
d)					
e)					
f)					

IMM 1295 VP-P (10-89) B

This form has been established by the Minister of Employment and Immigration
Formulaire établi par le Ministre de l'Emploi et de l'Immigration

Canada

11. My present occupation is – *Profession actuelle*	12. I have held my present job for *J'occupe mon emploi actuel depuis*	Months *Mois*	Years *An(s)*

13. The name and address of my employer and the type of business are – *Nom et adresse de mon employeur (préciser également le genre d'entreprise)*

14. The name and address of my prospective employer in Canada are: (Attach original copy of offer of employment)
Nom et adresse de mon employeur éventuel au Canada (joindre l'original de l'offre d'emploi)

15. My occupation in Canada will be – *Ma profession au Canada sera*	16. My salary will be – *Mon salaire sera de* $ Cdn. $ (en dollars canadiens)

17. I am expected to start my employment on *Je suis censé commencer à travailler le* ▶	D-J	M	Y-A	18. My employment is expected to finish on *Il est prévu que mon emploi prendra fin le* ▶	D-J	M	Y-A

19. Have you or any member of your family ever:
Les questions suivantes s'adressent également au visiteur et à tout membre de sa famille

("x" the appropriate box)
(*Inscrire "x" dans la case appropriée*)

a) Been treated for any serious physical or mental disorders or any communicable or chronic diseases ?
Vous a-t-on jamais traité(e) pour une maladie mentale ou physique grave, ou pour une maladie contagieuse ou chronique ? ☐ Yes *Oui* ☐ No *Non*

b) Been convicted of any crime in any country ?
Vous a-t-on jamais trouvé(e) coupable d'un acte criminel dans quelque pays que ce soit ? ☐ Yes *Oui* ☐ No *Non*

c) Been refused admission to or ordered to leave Canada ?
Vous a-t-on jamais refusé l'admission au Canada ou enjoint de quitter le Canada ? ☐ Yes *Oui* ☐ No *Non*

d) Been refused a visa to travel to Canada ?
Vous a-t-on jamais refusé l'autorisation de séjour au Canada ? ☐ Yes *Oui* ☐ No *Non*

e) Obtained a Canadian Social Insurance Number ?
Vous a-t-on jamais attribué un numéro d'assurance sociale au Canada ? ☐ Yes *Oui* ☐ No *Non*

f) In periods of either peace or war, have you ever been involved in the commission of a war crime or crime against humanity, such as: willful killing, torture, attacks upon, enslavement, starvation or other inhumane acts committed against civilians or prisoners of war; or deportation of civilians ?
En période de paix ou de guerre, avez-vous déjà participé à la commission d'un crime de guerre ou d'un crime contre l'humanité, c'est-à-dire de tout acte inhumain commis contre des populations civiles ou des prisonniers de guerre, par exemple, l'assassinat, la torture, l'agression, la réduction en esclavage ou la privation de nourriture, etc., ou encore participé à la déportation de civils ? ☐ Yes *Oui* ☐ No *Non*

If the answer to any of the above is "yes", give details below – *Si vous avez répondu "oui" à l'une ou l'autre question ci-dessus, veuillez donner les précisions*

20. During the past five years have you or any family member accompanying you lived in any other country for more than six months ?
Au cours des derniers cinq ans, avez-vous vécu dans un autre pays pendant plus de six mois ? Ne pas oublier les membres de votre famille qui vous accompagneront au Canada ▶ ☐ Yes *Oui* ☐ No *Non*

21. If answer to question 20 is "yes" list countries and length of stay
Si la réponse au 20 est affirmative, indiquer le nom de ces pays et la durée du séjour

Country – *Pays*	Length of Stay *Durée du séjour*	Country – *Pays*	Length of Stay *Durée du séjour*

I declare that I have answered all required questions in this application fully and truthfully
Je déclare avoir donné des réponses exactes et complètes à toutes les questions de la présente demande

Signature of Applicant – *Signature du requérant*   Date

172

Appendix 6-B

			DOCUMENT CHECKLIST
▌◆▌	Citizenship and Immigration Canada	Citoyenneté et Immigration Canada	APPLICATION TO CHANGE TERMS AND CONDITIONS OR EXTEND MY STAY IN CANADA

PUT AN " X " IN THE BOX IF YOU
SENT THE DOCUMENT. PHOTOCOPIES
MAY BE DESTROYED

ENCLOSE **PHOTOCOPIES** OF THE FOLLOWING DOCUMENTS

A)   FOR **EACH PERSON** INCLUDED IN THE APPLICATION APPLYING FOR AN EXTENSION OF HIS/HER **VISITOR STATUS**

　　1)　PASSPORT PAGES SHOWING THE PASSPORT NUMBER, NAME, DATE OF BIRTH, DATE PASSPORT ISSUED/EXPIRY DATE, AND STAMP MADE BY CANADIAN AUTHORITIES ON HIS/HER MOST RECENT ENTRY INTO CANADA. ☐

　　2)　CURRENT IMMIGRATION DOCUMENT. (IF YOU HAVE ONE) ☐

　　3)　VALID RETURN TICKET. ☐

　　4)　PROOF OF FUNDS AVAILABLE (BANK STATEMENT - MUST INDICATE CLIENT'S NAME AND ACCOUNT NUMBER; GUARANTOR'S LETTER; ETC) ☐

　　5)　ONE PASSPORT-SIZED PHOTOGRAPH. ☐

B)   FOR **EACH PERSON** INCLUDED IN THE APPLICATION APPLYING FOR AN EXTENSION OF HIS/HER **STUDENT AUTHORIZATION** *

　　1)　PASSPORT PAGES SHOWING THE PASSPORT NUMBER, NAME, DATE OF BIRTH, DATE PASSPORT ISSUED/EXPIRY DATE, AND STAMP MADE BY CANADIAN AUTHORITIES ON HIS/HER MOST RECENT ENTRY INTO CANADA. ☐

　　2)　CURRENT IMMIGRATION DOCUMENT. ☐

　　3)　LETTER OF ACCEPTANCE OR PROOF OF REGISTRATION FROM AN EDUCATIONAL INSTITUTION. * ☐

　　4)　PROOF OF FUNDS AVAILABLE (BANK STATEMENT - MUST INDICATE CLIENT'S NAME AND ACCOUNT NUMBER; GUARANTOR'S LETTER; ETC.) ☐

C)   FOR **EACH PERSON** INCLUDED IN THE APPLICATION APPLYING FOR AN EXTENSION OF HIS/HER **EMPLOYMENT AUTHORIZATION** *

　　1)　PASSPORT PAGES SHOWING THE PASSPORT NUMBER, NAME, DATE OF BIRTH, DATE PASSPORT ISSUED/EXPIRY DATE, AND STAMP MADE BY CANADIAN AUTHORITIES ON HIS/HER MOST RECENT ENTRY INTO CANADA. ☐

　　2)　CURRENT IMMIGRATION DOCUMENT. ☐

　　3)　JOB OFFER VALIDATION * AND/OR "JOB OFFER" LETTER FROM THE EMPLOYER. ☐

D)   FOR **EACH PERSON** INCLUDED IN THE APPLICATION APPLYING FOR AN EXTENSION OF HIS/HER **MINISTER'S PERMIT**

　　1)　DOCUMENTS RELATED TO THEIR REQUEST AS TOURISTS, STUDENTS OR WORKERS. ☐

　　2)　**TWO** (2) PASSPORT-SIZED PHOTOGRAPHS. ☐

*　IF YOU WORK OR STUDY IN THE PROVINCE OF QUEBEC, YOU MUST ALSO PROVIDE A CERTIFICAT D'ACCEPTATION DU QUÉBEC (CAQ). REFER TO THE GUIDEBOOK FOR EXEMPTION.

**COMPLETED APPLICATION WITH APPROPRIATE FEE MUST BE
RECEIVED AT IMMIGRATION CANADA WITHIN THE VALIDITY OF YOUR STATUS**

IMM 5288 (05-94) B

Canada

I✦I Citizenship and   Citoyenneté et
Immigration Canada   Immigration Canada

PROTECTED WHEN COMPLETED - A
PROTÉGÉ UNE FOIS REMPLI

CHANGE OF ADDRESS / INFORMATION NOTICE
AVIS DE CHANGEMENT D'ADRESSE OU DE MODIFICATION DES RENSEIGNEMENTS

HOW TO FILL OUT THIS NOTICE:

- Enter your name, client ID number and other personal details in **SECTION 1**.

- If you are moving, use **SECTION 2** to provide your new address and date you will be moving.

- Use **SECTION 3** if any information on your application form has changed.

- Mail to: **Case Processing Centre (CPC)**
     6212 - 55 Avenue
     Vegreville, AB
     T9C 1W5

COMMENT REMPLIR CET AVIS

- *Inscrire votre numéro d'identification du client, votre nom et autres renseignements personnels dans la PARTIE 1.*

- *Si vous déménagez, utiliser la PARTIE 2 pour indiquer votre nouvelle adresse et la date du déménagement.*

- *Utiliser la PARTIE 3 pour nous faire part de tout changement dans les renseignements fournis dans votre demande.*

- *Poster au : Centre de traitement des demandes (CTD)*
     6212, 55ᵉ avenue
     Vegreville, AB
     T9C 1W5

THE INFORMATION ON THIS FORM IS COLLECTED UNDER THE AUTHORITY OF THE CANADA IMMIGRATION ACT FOR THE PURPOSE OF KEEPING YOUR FILE UP-TO-DATE. THIS INFORMATION WILL BE RETAINED IN PERSONAL INFORMATION BANKS NUMBER EIC PPU 225, 285, 295 and/or 300. IT IS PROTECTED UNDER THE PROVISIONS OF THE PRIVACY ACT AND IS ACCESSIBLE TO YOU UPON REQUEST.
LA LOI SUR L'IMMIGRATION DU CANADA NOUS AUTORISE À RECUEILLIR LES RENSEIGNEMENTS DEMANDÉS CI-APRÈS EN VUE DE GARDER VOTRE DOSSIER À JOUR. LES RENSEIGNEMENTS QUE VOUS FOURNISSEZ SERONT VERSÉS AUX FICHIERS DE RENSEIGNEMENTS PERSONNELS Nº EIC PPU 225, 285, 295 et/ou 300. ILS SONT PROTÉGÉS PAR LA LOI SUR LA PROTECTION DES RENSEIGNEMENTS PERSONNELS ET VOUS POUVEZ LES CONSULTER SUR DEMANDE.

1. PERSONAL INFORMATION - *RENSEIGNEMENTS PERSONNELS*

Client File Number (shown on previous correspondence with you) *Numéro de dossier du client (Indiqué sur de la correspondance antérieure)*	Family Name - *Nom de famille*
	Given Name(s) - *Prénom(s)*

Date of Birth - *Date de naissance*	Country of Birth - *Pays de naissance*	Sex - *Sexe*
D - J M Y - A		☐ Male *Homme* ☐ Female *Femme*

2. NEW ADDRESS - *NOUVELLE ADRESSE*

Starting - *À compter du*	No. & Street - *Nº et rue*	Apt. No. *Nº d'app.*
D - J M Y - A		

City - *Ville*	Province - *Province*	Postal Code - *Code postal*

Telephone No. - *Nº de téléphone*	Telephone No. - *Nº de téléphone*
Home *Domicile* ▸ Area Code *Ind. rég.*	Business *Travail* ▸ Area Code *Ind. rég.*

3. IF ANY OF THE INFORMATION ON YOUR APPLICATION FORM CHANGES, PLEASE PUT AN X IN THE CORRECT BOX AND PROVIDE DETAILS IN THE SPACE BELOW.
SI L'UN DES RENSEIGNEMENTS QUE VOUS AVEZ FOURNIS DANS VOTRE FORMULAIRE DE DEMANDE A CHANGÉ, INSCRIRE UN «X» DANS LA CASE APPROPRIÉE ET FOURNIR DES PRÉCISIONS DANS L'ESPACE PRÉVU À CETTE FIN.

A ☐ My dependants have joined me in Canada.
    Les personnes à ma charge m'ont rejoint(e) au Canada.

B ☐ I have been charged with a criminal offence.
    J'ai été accusé(e) d'une infraction criminelle.

C ☐ I am no longer living with my sponsor.
    Je ne vis plus avec mon répondant.

D ☐ My marital status has changed.
    Mon état matrimonial a changé.

E ☐ I have had a baby.
    J'ai eu un enfant.

F ☐ I am leaving Canada for an indefinite period of time.
    Je quitte le Canada pour une période indéterminée.

G ☐ Other.
    Autre ▸ _____

Details - *Précisions*

IMM 5260 (06-94) B

Canada

I✦I Citizenship and   Citoyenneté et
Immigration Canada   Immigration Canada

PROTECTED WHEN COMPLETED - B

| FOR OFFICE USE ONLY |
| CLIENT ID NUMBER |

APPLICATION TO CHANGE TERMS AND CONDITIONS OR EXTEND MY STAY IN CANADA

I AM APPLYING FOR A: "A" ☐ VISITOR / TOURIST EXTENSION   "B" ☐ STUDENT AUTHORIZATION   "C" ☐ EMPLOYMENT AUTHORIZATION   "D" ☐ MINISTER'S PERMIT EXTENSION

NOTE: The required fee accompanying this application does not guarantee its acceptance

A - PERSONAL INFORMATION

1 SURNAME (FAMILY NAME)	GIVEN NAMES

OTHER NAMES USED	SEX
	☐ MALE ☐ FEMALE

	D	M	Y	PLACE OF BIRTH (CITY, STATE/PROVINCE AND COUNTRY)
DATE OF BIRTH				

CITIZEN OF	COUNTRY OF LAST PERMANENT RESIDENCE
	☐ SINCE BIRTH ☐ SINCE 19 ___

MARITAL STATUS ▶ ☐ NEVER MARRIED   ☐ ENGAGED   ☐ MARRIED   ▶ IF YOU ARE MARRIED, IS YOUR SPOUSE A CANADIAN CITIZEN OR PERMANENT RESIDENT?   ☐ YES   ☐ NO   ☐ WIDOWED   ☐ SEPARATED   ☐ DIVORCED

COMPLETE RESIDENTIAL ADDRESS IN MY HOME COUNTRY	COMPLETE MAILING ADDRESS IN CANADA
NO., STREET AND APT. NO.	NO., STREET AND APT. NO.
CITY COUNTRY POSTAL CODE	CITY PROVINCE

HOME TELEPHONE NUMBER:	AREA CODE		POSTAL CODE

TELEPHONE NUMBER IN CANADA FOR MESSAGES	AREA CODE	INDICATE MOST CONVENIENT TIME TO REACH YOU BY TELEPHONE	TIME _____ ☐ AM ☐ PM

B - MY FAMILY MEMBERS

2 SURNAME (FAMILY NAME)	GIVEN NAMES	RELATIONSHIP
DATE OF BIRTH D M Y COUNTRY OF BIRTH	CITIZENSHIP	IN CANADA ☐ YES ☐ NO TYPE OF DOCUMENT ☐ A ☐ B ☐ C ☐ D

3 SURNAME (FAMILY NAME)	GIVEN NAMES	RELATIONSHIP
DATE OF BIRTH D M Y COUNTRY OF BIRTH	CITIZENSHIP	IN CANADA ☐ YES ☐ NO TYPE OF DOCUMENT ☐ A ☐ B ☐ C ☐ D

4 SURNAME (FAMILY NAME)	GIVEN NAMES	RELATIONSHIP
DATE OF BIRTH D M Y COUNTRY OF BIRTH	CITIZENSHIP	IN CANADA ☐ YES ☐ NO TYPE OF DOCUMENT ☐ A ☐ B ☐ C ☐ D

5 SURNAME (FAMILY NAME)	GIVEN NAMES	RELATIONSHIP
DATE OF BIRTH D M Y COUNTRY OF BIRTH	CITIZENSHIP	IN CANADA ☐ YES ☐ NO TYPE OF DOCUMENT ☐ A ☐ B ☐ C ☐ D

6 SURNAME (FAMILY NAME)	GIVEN NAMES	RELATIONSHIP
DATE OF BIRTH D M Y COUNTRY OF BIRTH	CITIZENSHIP	IN CANADA ☐ YES ☐ NO TYPE OF DOCUMENT ☐ A ☐ B ☐ C ☐ D

IMM 1249 (05-94) E   (DISPONIBLE EN FRANÇAIS - IMM 1249 F)   **Canada**

C - MEDICAL EXAMINATIONS

PRINCIPAL APPLICANT AND FAMILY MEMBERS LISTED IN B	HAVE COMPLETED IMMIGRATION MEDICAL EXAMINATION REQUESTED BY CANADIAN AUTHORITIES		DID YOU/YOUR FAMILY MEMBERS TRAVEL DIRECTLY FROM YOUR HOME COUNTRY? IF NO, LIST COUNTRIES TRAVELLED THROUGH.
PRINCIPAL APPLICANT	☐ NO ☐ YES	DATE D M Y · · PLACE (CITY AND COUNTRY)	☐ YES ☐ NO
FIRST FAMILY MEMBER	☐ NO ☐ YES	DATE D M Y · · PLACE (CITY AND COUNTRY)	☐ YES ☐ NO
SECOND FAMILY MEMBER	☐ NO ☐ YES	DATE D M Y · · PLACE (CITY AND COUNTRY)	☐ YES ☐ NO
THIRD FAMILY MEMBER	☐ NO ☐ YES	DATE D M Y · · PLACE (CITY AND COUNTRY)	☐ YES ☐ NO
FOURTH FAMILY MEMBER	☐ NO ☐ YES	DATE D M Y · · PLACE (CITY AND COUNTRY)	☐ YES ☐ NO
FIFTH FAMILY MEMBER	☐ NO ☐ YES	DATE D M Y · · PLACE (CITY AND COUNTRY)	☐ YES ☐ NO

D - COMING INTO CANADA

| 6 | MOST RECENT ENTRY TO CANADA | PLACE ▶ | DATE D M Y | MY CURRENT STATUS IS VALID UNTIL | DATE D M Y |

| 7 | ORIGINAL ENTRY TO CANADA | PLACE ▶ | HAVE YOU LEFT CANADA SINCE YOUR ORIGINAL ENTRY? ☐ NO ☐ YES ▶ WHERE AND WHEN DID YOU RETURN TO CANADA | |
| | | DATE D M Y | PLACE DATE D M Y | |

| 8 | MY ORIGINAL REASON FOR COMING TO CANADA |

| 9 | MY DEPARTURE PLANS ARE |

10	HAVE YOU OR ANY OF YOUR DEPENDANTS REMAINED IN CANADA BEYOND THE VALIDITY OF YOUR STATUS?	☐ YES ☐ NO ▶ IF "YES" PLEASE COMPLETE SECTION F, QUESTION 18
11	HAVE YOU OR ANY OF YOUR DEPENDANTS ATTENDED SCHOOL IN CANADA?	☐ YES ☐ NO
	WAS AUTHORIZATION OBTAINED PRIOR TO BEGINNING STUDIES?	☐ YES ☐ NO ▶ IF "NO" PLEASE COMPLETE SECTION F, QUESTION 19
12	HAVE YOU OR ANY OF YOUR DEPENDANTS WORKED IN CANADA?	☐ YES ☐ NO
	WAS AUTHORIZATION OBTAINED PRIOR TO BEGINNING WORK?	☐ YES ☐ NO ▶ IF "NO" PLEASE COMPLETE SECTION F, QUESTION 20

E - MY REQUEST

| 13 | I WANT TO ▶ ☐ EXTEND MY STAY IN CANADA UNTIL | DATE D M Y | AND/OR ☐ CHANGE TERMS AND CONDITIONS |
| | FOR THE FOLLOWING REASONS: (Give complete details) |

14	TO SUPPORT MYSELF IN CANADA:	• I RECEIVE SUPPORT FROM:
	• I HAVE THE FOLLOWING : FUNDS AVAILABLE $ _____ CANADIAN DOLLARS	☐ SELF ☐ FRIEND / RELATIVE ☐ GENERAL WELFARE ASSISTANCE ☐ OTHER
	CREDIT CARD TYPE AND NUMBER ▶	EXPIRY DATE ▶

QUESTIONS 15, 16 AND 17 TO BE COMPLETED BY TOURISTS ONLY

| 15 | MY OCCUPATION IN MY HOME COUNTRY IS ▶ | 16 | MY EMPLOYER'S NAME AND ADDRESS IN MY HOME COUNTRY IS: |
| 17 | I HAVE TO RETURN TO WORK / SCHOOL BY ▶ | D M Y | |

F - ADDITIONAL INFORMATION

18	IF YOU OR YOUR DEPENDANTS REMAINED BEYOND THE VALIDITY OF YOUR STATUS PLEASE COMPLETE THE FOLLOWING:

PERSON'S NAME	PERSON'S NAME
EXPIRY DATE OF STATUS	EXPIRY DATE OF STATUS
LAST ENTERED CANADA ON D M Y AT (PLACE)	LAST ENTERED CANADA ON D M Y AT (PLACE)

19	IF YOU OR YOUR DEPENDANTS ATTENDED SCHOOL WITHOUT PERMISSION PLEASE COMPLETE THE FOLLOWING:

STUDENTS NAME	STUDENTS NAME
NAME OF SCHOOL ATTENDED	NAME OF SCHOOL ATTENDED
PERIOD OF STUDY START DATE D M Y LAST DATE D M Y	PERIOD OF STUDY START DATE D M Y LAST DATE D M Y

20	IF YOU OR YOUR DEPENDANTS WORKED WITHOUT PERMISSION PLEASE COMPLETE THE FOLLOWING:

WORKER'S NAME	WORKER'S NAME
NAME OF EMPLOYER /COMPANY	NAME OF EMPLOYER/COMPANY
ADDRESS	ADDRESS
PERIOD OF EMPLOYMENT START DATE D M Y LAST DATE D M Y	PERIOD OF EMPLOYMENT START DATE D M Y LAST DATE D M Y

21	IF YOU ANSWERED "YES" TO ANY OF THE ABOVE QUESTIONS, GIVE THE REASONS AND CIRCUMSTANCES CONCERNING YOUR SITUATION

22	HAVE YOU OR ANY OF YOUR DEPENDANTS IN CANADA EVER BEEN CONVICTED OF OR CHARGED WITH A CRIME OR OFFENCE IN ANY COUNTRY?	☐ YES ☐ NO

IF "YES" COMPLETE THE FOLLOWING SECTION. PLEASE ATTACH CERTIFICATE OF CONVICTION , PROBATION DOCUMENT OR ANY OTHER DOCUMENTS YOU POSSESS RELATING TO THE OFFENCE.

PERSON'S NAME	PERSON'S NAME
DATE AND PLACE OF CONVICTION	DATE AND PLACE OF CONVICTION
OFFENCE SENTENCE	OFFENCE SENTENCE

23	HAVE YOU OR ANY OF YOUR DEPENDANTS IN CANADA SUFFERED FROM ANY SERIOUS MENTAL OR PHYSICAL ILLNESS?	☐ YES ☐ NO

IF "YES" COMPLETE THE FOLLOWING SECTION.

PERSON'S NAME	PERSON'S NAME
NAME OF ILLNESS	NAME OF ILLNESS
PERIOD OF ILLNESS	PERIOD OF ILLNESS
TREATMENT RECEIVED	TREATMENT RECEIVED

G - DECLARATION

DECLARATION OF APPLICANT
I DECLARE THAT THE INFORMATION I HAVE GIVEN IN THIS APPLICATION IS TRUTHFUL, COMPLETE AND CORRECT. I UNDERSTAND THAT ANY STATEMENT OR CONCEALMENT OF A MATERIAL FACT MAY RESULT IN MY REMOVAL FROM CANADA.

_____
SIGNATURE OF APPLICANT

_____
DATE

FOR OFFICIAL USE ONLY

| CANADA IMMIGRATION DECISION | ▶ ☐ REQUEST AS DETAILED ABOVE IS APPROVED | ☐ REQUEST WITH CHANGES APPROVED | ☐ REQUEST REFUSED | ☐ INTERVIEW REQUIRED | ☐ A 27(2) REPORT |

COMMENTS

_____
SIGNATURE OF IMMIGRATION OFFICER

_____
DATE

THE INFORMATION YOU PROVIDE ON THIS DOCUMENT IS COLLECTED UNDER THE AUTHORITY OF THE *IMMIGRATION ACT* TO DETERMINE WHETHER THE TERMS AND CONDITIONS OF YOUR STAY SHOULD BE CHANGED OR WHETHER YOU SHOULD BE GRANTED AN EXTENSION. THIS INFORMATION WILL BE STORED IN PERSONAL INFORMATION BANKS NUMBER EIC PPU 225, 295 OR 300; IT IS PROTECTED AND YOU HAVE THE RIGHT OF ACCESS TO IT UNDER THE *PRIVACY ACT*.

Appendix 6-C

List of Types of Employment Authorization which may only be provided for you at a time.

a) "Volunteers without remuneration" destined to religious and charitable organizations (R20)(5)(e)(ii) VEC-E20 and E25);

b) Popular musicians (Musician, Instrumental 3332-130);

c) Participants in international student and young worker exchange programs (R20)(5)(e)(iii) VEC-E35). Note that, for certain programs, no extensions beyond either 6 or 12 months are to be granted. Refer to IS 15.17, programs descriptions to determine whether there are limitations on extensions.

d) All persons holding or being issued Minister's Permits;

e) Physicians, general practice 3111-166;

f) Participants in the Foreign Domestic Movement:

Housekeeper	6142-110
Companion	6142-126
Servant domestic	6142-130
Babysitter	6147-110
Children's nurse (nanny)	6147-114
Parent's helper	6147-130

g) Citizen of Countries for which the Visa, Information Telex (VIT) procedure is in effect, with the exception of Yugoslavia residents and nationals when dealt with in accordance with IC 2.20(6)(c)(i), IC 2.36 and IC 3.05(8)(b) and (c);

h) Persons who are being issued "open" employment authorizations with the following exceptions:

— Canadian Football players, coashes and their spouses may be issued authorizations for the length of the players' or coach's contract.

— Persons issued "open" employment authorizations under the provisions of IS 15.20

Appendix 6-D

Temporary Foreign Worker Processing Summary

All workers who are citizens or residents of the U.S.A., and the residents of Greenland and of St-Pierre-et-Miquelon, as well as all other workers who are exempted from employment validation, may apply at the border for an employment authorization (R19(3)(a)).

Unless specifically exempted, all workers are required to obtain an employment authorization and employment validation.

Those workers exempted from employment authorization are also exempted from employment validation and may be processed abroad, at the border, or in Canada, as any ordinary visitor.

TYPE OF WORKER	AUTHORIZATION		VALIDATION		MAY APPLY AT		QUEBEC CAQ NEEDED	MANUAL REFERENCE
	EXEMPT	NEEDED	EXEMPT	NEEDED	BORDER	IN CANADA		
Actor								
— Screen and T.V.		✓		✓	R19(3)(a) & (b)		✓	15.38(4)(d)
— Stage		✓	R20(5)(e)(iii) E99		R19(3)(a)(iv)	R19(4)(h)		15.38(4)(d)
Adjudicators (Dance & Music)	R19(1)(l)		✓		✓	✓		15.04(12)
Administrator		✓		✓			✓	
Administrator (Sports) — for Professional Canadian-Based Team		✓	R20(5)(e)(i) E19		R19(3)(a)(iv)	R19(4)(d)		15.15(3)(a)
Applicant-in-Canada — not yet disposed of		✓	R20(5)(a) A01			R19(4)(i)		
Appraisers		✓		✓			✓	

180

TYPE OF WORKER	AUTHORIZATION		VALIDATION		MAY APPLY AT		QUEBEC CAQ NEEDED	MANUAL REFERENCE
	EXEMPT	NEEDED	EXEMPT	NEEDED	BORDER	IN CANADA		
Associates — Research		✓		✓			✓	
Athletes — Amateur players and coaches (50% of earned income factor applies)		✓	R20(5)(a)(iii) E95		R19(3)(a)(iv)	R19(4)(d)		15.04(11)(c), 15.17(10)
Athletes — Individual Competition Participants	R19(1)(k)		✓		✓	✓		15.04(11)
Athletes — Players for Professional Canadian Team		✓	R20(5)(e)(iii) E99		R19(3)(a)(iv)	R19(4)(d)		
Athletes — Professionals — for Tryouts	✓		✓		✓	✓		15.04(1)
Athletic Trainers/Therapists		✓		✓		✓		
Auctioneers		✓		✓		✓		
Audio Technicians (Bands) — not incidental to commercial activity		✓	R20(5)(a) A08		R19(3)(a)(iv)	R19(4)(h)		
Auditor — Hired by Company Specifically for Audit		✓		✓			✓	

TYPE OF WORKER	AUTHORIZATION		VALIDATION			MAY APPLY AT		QUEBEC CAQ NEEDED	MANUAL REFERENCE
	EXEMPT	NEEDED	EXEMPT	NEEDED	BORDER	IN CANADA			
Auditors — Company Employees for Internal Audit	R19(1)(i)		✓		✓	✓			
Booth — for Promotion of Tourism and Sales to Wholesalers	R19(1)(h)		✓		✓	✓			
Buyers	R19(1)(g)								15.04(7)
Camp Counsellors		✓		✓				✓	
Camp Owners — (one of and spouse only and where no Canadian owner or co-owner)		✓	R20(5)(e)(i) E01		R19(3)(a)(iv)				
Caribbean Seasonal Workers		✓		✓				✓	15.41
Carnival Workers — not circus acts		✓		✓	✓				15.39
Circus Performers — less than 15 — Groups of 15 or more	R19(1)(d)	✓	R20(5)(a) A08 ✓		R19(3)(a)(iv) ✓	R19(4)(f) ✓			
Civilian Component	R19(1)(b)		✓		✓	✓			
Clergy (to perform religious duties)	R19(1)(c)		✓		✓	✓			15.04(3)
Clinical Clerks	R19(1)(s)		✓		✓	✓			

TYPE OF WORKER	AUTHORIZATION EXEMPT	AUTHORIZATION NEEDED	VALIDATION EXEMPT	VALIDATION NEEDED	MAY APPLY AT BORDER	MAY APPLY AT IN CANADA	QUEBEC CAQ NEEDED	MANUAL REFERENCE
Coach								
— Canadian Amateur or Semi-pro Team		✓	R20(5)(e)(iii) E99		R19(3)(a)(iv)	R19(4)(d)		15.04(11)(c)
— Canadian Professional Team		✓	R20(5)(e)(iii) E99		R19(3)(a)(iv)	R19(4)(d)		
Coin/Stamp Collectors								
— At Conventions	✓		✓		✓	✓		15.55
— Other than at Conventicns		✓	R20(5)(e)(i) E05		R19(3)(a)(iv)		✓	15.55
Company Expert	R19(1)(j)		✓			✓		
Consultant		✓		✓	R19(3)(a), (b)	✓		
Convention Attendants	✓		✓		✓	✓		
Convention Organizers — Organizing Company Personnel Only	R19(1)(u)		✓		✓	✓		
Convention Refugee — not yet Permanent Resident		✓	R20(5)(a) A02			R19(4)(k)(ii)		
Corporation & Union Personnel — to consult, monitor, inspect at parent, subsidiary or branch office	R19(1)(i)							15.04(9)
Correspondents (News)	R19(1)(f)		✓		✓	✓		

TYPE OF WORKER	AUTHORIZATION		VALIDATION		MAY APPLY AT		QUEBEC CAQ NEEDED	MANUAL REFERENCE
	EXEMPT	NEEDED	EXEMPT	NEEDED	BORDER	IN CANADA		
Crew Member — of vehicle for International Transport	R19(1)(e)							15.04(5)
Dancer — Ballet & Classical, etc. — Exotic		✓	R20(5)(e)(iii) E99 R20(5)(e)(iii) E99		R19(3)(a)(iv) R19(3)(a)(iv)	R19(4)(h) R19(4)(h)		
Dentists		✓		✓	R19(3)(a), (b)		✓	
Dependent of: — Diplomats — Visiting Forces Act — Other Government Officials		✓	R20(5)(e)(iii) E99			R19(4)(h)		15.20(2)
Diplomat	R19(1)(a)		✓		✓	✓		15.04
Directors (stage, artistic)		✓	R20(5)(e)(iii) E99		R19(3)(a)(iv)	R19(4)(h)		15.38(4)(f)
Doctors (M.D.)		✓		✓	R19(3)(a), (b)			
Dog Handlers — Coming with Own Foreign Dog Only	R19(1)(k)		✓		✓	✓		
Drivers — Racing Cars	R19(1)(k)		✓		✓	✓		
Emergency Repair Workers		✓	R20(5)(a) A09		R19(3)(a)(iv)	R19(4)(f)		
Emergency Workers	R19(1)(j)		✓		✓			
Eminent Individuals		✓	R20(5)(e)(iii) E40		R19(3)(a)(iv)			

TYPE OF WORKER	AUTHORIZATION		VALIDATION		MAY APPLY AT		QUEBEC CAQ NEEDED	MANUAL REFERENCE
	EXEMPT	NEEDED	EXEMPT	NEEDED	BORDER	IN CANADA		
Entertainer (see Specific Category) — Actor, Musician, Dancer, Singer								
Evaluators		✓		✓	R19(3)(a), (b)			
Examiners	R19(1)(n)		✓		✓	✓		
Exotic Dancer (See Dancer Exotic)								
Expert Witness	R19(1)(p)							15.04(16)
Fellowship Holders		✓	R20(5)(e)(iii) E45		✓			15.17(8)
Field Servicemen — warranty — familiarization & repairs		✓	R20(5)(e)(i) E10		✓			15.15(3)(d)
Fishing Guides		✓		✓	R19(3)(a)		✓	15.49, App. N
Graduate Assistants		✓	R20(5)(e)(iii) E45		R19(3)(a)(iv)			
Guards (Security)		✓		✓	R19(3)(a), (b)		✓	
Guest Lecturers		✓	R20(5)(e)(iii) E40		R19(3)(a)(iv)			
Guest Speakers	✓		✓		✓	✓		
Hobbyists	✓		✓		✓	✓		
Household Service (Relative from Abroad)	✓		✓		✓	✓		
Household Service Worker		✓		✓	R19(3)(a), (b)			

TYPE OF WORKER	AUTHORIZATION		VALIDATION		MAY APPLY AT		QUEBEC CAQ NEEDED	MANUAL REFERENCE
	EXEMPT	NEEDED	EXEMPT	NEEDED	BORDER	IN CANADA		
Incentive Meeting — see Conventions / Installation to Equipment								
Installers		✓		✓	R19(3)(a), (b)			
Interns		✓		✓	R19(3)(a), (b)			
Intra-Company Transferee — See Definition at Reference		✓	R20(5)(e)(i) E15		R19(3)(a)(iv)			
Jockeys (and Agents)	R19(1)(k)		✓		✓	✓		
Judges — Animal and Agricultural Competitions	R19(1)(m)		✓		✓	✓		
Lecturers (Guest)		✓	R20(5)(e)(iii), E40		R19(3)(a)(iv)			
Long Term Illegals — Applicants in Canaada		✓	R20(5)(a) A01			R19(4)(i)		
Medical Elective	R19(1)(s)		✓		✓	✓		
Mexican Seasonal Workers		✓		✓			✓	15.41
Military Personnel — Visiting Forces only	R19(1)(b)		✓		✓	✓		
Minister's Permit Holder		✓				R19(4)(e)		

TYPE OF WORKER	AUTHORIZATION EXEMPT	AUTHORIZATION NEEDED	VALIDATION EXEMPT	VALIDATION NEEDED	MAY APPLY AT BORDER	MAY APPLY AT IN CANADA	QUEBEC CAQ NEEDED	MANUAL REFERENCE
Ministerial Approved Program		✓	R20(5)(d) D10		✓			15.12(1)
Musical Groups (Performing Arts)	R19(1)(d)							
— 15 or more in group		✓	R20(5)(a) A08	✓	R19(3)(a)(iv)	✓ R19(4)(h)	✓	15.38(3)(a) 15.38(3)(b) 15.38(3)(c)
— less than 15 (Entertainers)		✓						
News Correspondents	R19(1)(f)		✓		✓	✓		
News Reporting Crews	R19(1)(f)		✓		✓	✓		
Personal Servants — with usual employer	R19(1)(q)							15.04(17)
Physicians		✓		✓	R19(3)(a), (b)			
Post Doctoral Fellows		✓	R20(5)(e)(iii) E45		R19(3)(a)(iv)			
Professors (Visiting)		✓	R20(5)(e)(iii) E40		R19(3)(a)(iv)			
Program Evaluators		✓		✓	R19(3)(a), (b)		✓	
Racing Stable Personnel — Canadian stable		✓	✓		R19(3)(a), (b) ✓	✓	✓	
— Foreign Stable	R19(1)(k)	✓		✓	✓			
Railroad Track Maintenance Crew — rail grinding — ballast cleaning — rail inspecting		✓	R20(5)(e)(i) E10		✓			15.08(E)(I)(iii)(b)
Recruiters (Amway, etc.)		✓	R20(5)(e)(i) E19		R19(3)(a)(iv)			

TYPE OF WORKER	AUTHORIZATION		VALIDATION		MAY APPLY AT		QUEBEC CAQ NEEDED	MANUAL REFERENCE
	EXEMPT	NEEDED	EXEMPT	NEEDED	BORDER	IN CANADA		
Referees — Canadian Competition — International Meet	R19(1)(L)	✓	✓	✓	R19(3)(a), (b) ✓	✓	✓	
Religious Workers	R19(1)(c)		✓		✓	✓		
Removal Order that is Stayed or cannot be Executed		✓	R20(5)(a) A04–A07			R19(4)(k)		15.08(A)(2)
Repair Personnel — Emergency Situation — Warranty (Familiarization and Repairs)		✓ ✓	R20(5)(a) A09 R20(5)(e)(i) E10		R19(3)(a)(iv) R19(3)(a)(iv)	R19(4)(f)		
Reporters (News)	R19(1)(f)	✓	✓		✓			
Research Associates		✓		✓	✓		✓	
Sales Representatives — to Wholesalers, Retailers, Businesses and Institutions Only	R19(1)(h)		✓		✓			
Security Guards — general — El Al Airline		✓ ✓	✓	✓	R19(3)(a), (b) R19(3)		✓	15.43

TYPE OF WORKER	AUTHORIZATION		VALIDATION		MAY APPLY AT		QUEBEC CAQ NEEDED	MANUAL REFERENCE
	EXEMPT	NEEDED	EXEMPT	NEEDED	BORDER	IN CANADA		
Self-employed Persons — To establish business in Canada		✓	R20(5)(e)(i) E01 — Canadian recruits E05 — significant benefits		✓			15.15(1)(a), (c)
Seminar Leaders		✓		✓	R19(3)(a), (b)		✓	
Service Personnel — See Repair Personnel								
Singer (See Musical Groups)								
Speakers (Guest)	R19(1)(o)		✓		✓	✓		
Spouses of Fellowship Holders — UK & Australia		✓	R20(5)(e)(iii) E45			R19(4)(c)		
Students (CIDA)		✓	R20(5)(d) D30			R19(4)(b)		15.12(3)
Studuents (Destitute)		✓	R20(5)(c) C05			R19(4)(b)		15.11
Supervisors		✓	R20(5)(e)(i) E10		R19(3)(a)(iv)			
Surgeons		✓		✓	R19(3)(a), (b)		✓	
Teachers (Exchange Programs)		✓	R20(5)(e)(iii) E40		✓			15.17(7)
Theatre Technical Staff		✓		✓	R19(3)(a), (b)		✓	
Tobacco/Specialists (Curers)		✓		✓	R19(3)(a), (b)		✓	

TYPE OF WORKER	AUTHORIZATION		VALIDATION		MAY APPLY AT		QUEBEC CAQ NEEDED	MANUAL REFERENCE
	EXEMPT	NEEDED	EXEMPT	NEEDED	BORDER	IN CANADA		
Tobacco Exchange Worker		✓	R20(5)(e)(iii) E35		R19(3)(a)(iv)			
Trainees (Not "Hands On") (Intra Industry)	R19(1)(t)		✓		✓	✓		
Trainers (Company Employees for Company Personnel)		✓	R20(5)(e)(i) E19		R19(3)(a)(iv)			
Trainers (General)		✓		✓	R19(3)(a), (b)		✓	
Transferees (Intra-Company)		✓	R20(5)(e)(i) E15		R19(3)(a)(iv)			
Tour Guides								15.50
Travelogue Personnel — three or less for six weeks or less		✓	R20(5)(e)(i) E19		R19(3)(a), (b)			15.04(6)
— three or more for six weeks or more		✓		✓	R19(3)(a), (b)		✓	15.04(6)
Umpires (see Referees)								
Visiting Professors		✓	R20(5)(e)(iii) E40		R19(3)(a)(iv)			
Volunteer — non-religious duties		✓	R20(5)(e)(ii) E20, E25		✓			15.16(3), (4)
Working Holiday Participants		✓	R20(5)(e)(iii), E35		R19(3)(a)(iv)			

7

TEMPORARY ENTRY INTO CANADA: EMPLOYMENT VALIDATIONS

7.1 INTRODUCTION

This chapter addresses the manner in which foreign workers may apply for an employment authorization where the applications do not fall within the specific categories or exemptions listed in the preceding chapters of this book.

In order to qualify for an employment authorization under this general category, applicants would first be required to apply for a Foreign Worker Record (also referred to as employment validation) at a Canada Employment Centre ("CEC") and, if successful, would be in a position to apply for an employment authorization at a processing post.

7.2 LEGISLATIVE BASIS FOR ISSUING VALIDATIONS

The legislative authority for making an application for an employment validation at a CEC is found in both immigration and employment legislation.

7.2.1 IMMIGRATION LEGISLATION

The *Immigration Regulations (Regulations)* and immigration policy provide a basis for conferral between immigration officers and employment counsellors.

(a) Regulations

Section 20(1) of the *Regulations* states as follows:

> An immigration officer shall not issue an employment authorization to a person if,

(a) in his opinion, employment of the person in Canada will adversely affect employment opportunities for Canadian citizens or permanent residents in Canada . . .

Section 20(3) of the *Regulations* provides an objective basis for reviewing whether Canadian citizens and permanent residents will suffer an adverse effect by the presence of foreign workers in Canada.

In considering whether employment of prospective foreign workers will have an adverse "effect" on the job opportunities for Canadian citizens and permanent residents, immigration officers are required to consider the following criteria:

1. Whether the prospective employer has made reasonable efforts to hire or train Canadian citizens or permanent residents for the employment with respect to which an employment authorization is sought.

2. The qualifications and experience of the applicant for the employment for which the employment authorization is sought;

3. Whether the wages and working conditions offered are sufficient to attract and retain employment of Canadian citizens or permanent residents.

Given the fact that the immigration officer's expertise is not in the area of employment policies and procedures, section 20(4) of the *Regulations* places an obligation on the immigration officer to take into consideration the "opinion" of the officer of the National Employment Service, serving the area in which the person seeking an employment authorization wishes to engage in employment. The National Employment Service has established the Canada Employment Centre, which, *inter alia*, is entrusted with the responsibility to consider the questions set out in section 20(3)(a)(b) and (c) of the *Regulations* in relation to applications for temporary entry to Canada (employment authorizations). The function of the CEC is to administer the various policies and programs of the National Employment Service. Employment counsellors at the CEC are entrusted with the responsibility to provide opinions to the immigration officer in relation to whether a person seeking an employment authorization meets the criteria specified in section 20(1) and (3) of the *Regulations*. In practice, however, these "opinions" are the *de facto* authorization which allows the immigration officer to issue an employment authorization if the applicant meets all other criteria under the *Immigration Act (Act)*.

While there is an obvious legislative basis for the relationship between the CEC and the processing posts in relation to the issuance of employment validations, the system established between processing posts responsible for the decision-making pertaining to the application for a work permit and the National Employment Service has been largely initiated by various policy directives.

192

(b) Existence of a Labour Dispute

Immigration officers are not authorized to issue an employment authorization to a person if the issuance of the employment authorization will affect:

1.   the settlement of any labour dispute that is in progress at the place or intended place of employment, or

2.   the employment of any person who is involved in such a dispute.

(See section 21(b) of the *Regulations*.)

(c) Immigration Policy

Section 15.01(2) of the *Immigration Manual* reinforces that "adverse effect" relates not only to lack of Canadian citizens and permanent residents able to fill a vacancy but, as well, the efforts of the prospective employer in training Canadian citizens and permanent residents so as to ensure that there is not a continuing dependency on foreign workers which can be remedied by proper training.

Section 15.01(3) of the *Immigration Manual* emphasizes that the immigration officer, in determining whether the employment authorization will be issued to an applicant, will consider whether the application complies with all the statutory requirements, including the "adverse effects" determination. In order to form an opinion in relation to "adverse effects", the immigration officer must be informed by the labour market group (i.e., Employment Counsellors at the CEC, also known as Foreign Recruitment) on the effect of the foreign worker on the employment opportunities of Canadian citizens or permanent residents based on the status of the labour market in a certain area or occupation. The *Immigration Manual* also clarifies that the process whereby the labour market group informs the immigration officer of the status of the labour market in certain areas or occupations in order that the immigration officer might form an opinion, on the effect of the entry of the foreign worker and the employment opportunities of Canadians or permanent residents, is referred to as an "Employment Validation".

Section 15.01(4) of the *Immigration Manual* stipulates that it is the employer's responsibility to obtain an Employment Validation prior to sponsoring the entry of the foreign worker to Canada for purposes of filling a vacancy. Once it is established that the employment opportunities of Canadian citizens and permanent residents will not be adversely affected by the admission of the foreign worker, the job offer will be "validated".

Job offers are normally validated through the issuance of a Foreign Worker Record (transmittal of information to processing posts is done electronically as particularized below), although it is possible to obtain validations in other formats such as a letter which authorizes the entry of a large number of employees by way of a ''bulk'' validation approval.

If the Foreign Recruitment Employment Counsellor refuses to validate the job offer made by an employer to the foreign worker, the immigration officer would normally deny the Application for Temporary Entry to Canada (Employment Authorization), as the refusal of the validation would result in a negative ''opinion'' as to the adverse effects and, therefore, as to the issuance of an employment authorization.

Given the length of time which is involved in obtaining an employment authorization, in cases of urgency, section 19(3) of the *Act* (i.e., discretionary entry of inadmissible persons not exceeding 30 days) can be utilized in order to expedite the entry of a foreign worker.

7.2.2 EMPLOYMENT LEGISLATION

(a) Statutory Law

The legislative basis for the services provided by the National Employment Service to employers wishing to recruit foreign workers is found in section 5 of the *Employment and Immigration Department and Commission Act*, R.S.C. 1985, c. E-5, which states:

> The powers, duties and functions of the Minister extend to and include all matters . . . relating to:
>
> (a) the development and utilization of labour market resources in Canada;
>
> (b) employment services;
>
> (c) unemployment insurance; and
>
> (d) immigration.

In addition, section 120 of the *Unemployment Insurance Act*, R.S.C. 1985, c. U-1 (Part VI National Employment Service) states as follows:

> The commission shall continue and maintain a national employment service to assist workers to find suitable employment and employers to find suitable workers.

In addition to the foregoing, section 4 of the *National Employment Service Regulations*, C.R.C. 1978, c. 1573 states as follows:

> The aim of the employment service is the organization of the labour market as an integral part of a program for the achievement and maintenance of the highest possible level of employment.

194

Subsection 8(2) of the *National Employment Services Regulations* lists the duties of the Employment Service as follows:

> The Employment Service shall assist employers to find suitable workers by
>
> (a) assisting employers in solving manpower planning and recruitment problems on a short and long term basis;
>
> (b) obtaining from the employers information on job vacancies;
>
> (c) searching for workers in Canada and elsewhere; and
>
> (d) advising employers on various ways to meet manpower needs.

Accordingly, the basis for the involvement of the employment branch of the Ministry of Human Resources has been clearly substantiated by the foregoing.

(b) Employment Policy

The policy basis for the involvement of the National Employment Service in relation to the approval of the entry of foreign workers is found in Chapter 17 of the *Employment Manual*, entitled "Foreign Worker Recruitment". The purpose of Chapter 17 is to set out the policies and procedures of the National Employment Service as they relate to the admission of foreign workers to Canada. As such, it is the most significant basis for the authority of the National Employment Service in relation to validating offers of employment to foreign workers. Chapter 17 offers a comprehensive explanation of the role of employment counsellors in relation to the entry of foreign workers to Canada and offers step-by-step guidance to employment counsellors.

7.3 RESPONSIBILITY OF EMPLOYMENT COUNSELLORS

Employment counsellors are responsible for validating offers of employment to foreign workers. When validating offers of employment they are required to take the following steps:

1. briefly outline the CEC's foreign worker policy including user fees;

2. the CEC will help the employer determine if the vacancy is permanent or temporary;

3. if the vacancy is temporary, consider whether it falls within the category that:

(a)   is exempt from the employment authorization requirement; or

(b)   is contained in the validation exemption categories.

If the job vacancy falls into one of the above categories, the matter should be referred to the immigration officer for further advise and guidance. Counsellors may contact the immigration officer on behalf of the employer.

If the employment counsellor requires validation, the CEC will require the employer to advertise and or obtain the assistance of the CEC to find a qualified Canadian to perform the job. If there are no qualified Canadians available to perform the job, the counsellor will commence the validation process.

7.4 DEFINITION OF EMPLOYMENT VALIDATION

Section 15.01(3) of the *Immigration Manual* defines an Employment Validation as the process which "entails the Labour Market Group informing the immigration officer of the status of the labour market in a certain area or occupation in order that the immigration officer might form an opinion, as required by the *Regulations* on the effect of the entry of a foreign worker on the employment opportunities of Canadians or permanent residents". The National Employment Service oversees the CECs which, in turn, hire the Foreign Worker Recruitment Employment Counsellors.

According to section 17.03 of the *Employment Manual*, a "Temporary Employment Validation" refers to the favourable opinion given by an officer of the National Employment Service to an immigration or visa officer on the questions referred to in subsection 20(3) of the *Regulations*.

The Foreign Worker Recruitment Operational Guidelines, Employer Services Programs and Services, Ontario Region, 1992, define a "validation" as follows:

> An on-line document of the offer of employment by the Canada Employment Centre. It is used to advise immigration that the recruitment of a foreign worker by the employer will not adversely effect employment and career opportunities of Canadians.

7.4.1 "CANADIANS FIRST" POLICY

The "Canadians First" policy is expressly noted in section 17.04 of the *Employment Manual* as follows:

> Only Canadians Citizens or permanent residents have a *right* to work in Canada. This is sometimes referred to as the 'Canadians First' Policy

Notwithstanding the "Canadians First" policy, Canadian employment policy encourages the recruitment of foreign workers if the employment of a foreign worker will not adversely affect employment and career opportunities for Canadians or permanent residents in Canada and/or will increase employment for the Canadian domestic workforce; and where it has been determined that:

1. working conditions offered are sufficient to attract and retain in employment Canadian citizens and permanent residents;

2. the employment of the foreign worker will not affect the settlement of any labour dispute, or the employment of any person who is involved in such a dispute at the place or intended place of employment; and

3. the job offer itself is *bona fide* or is designed to be accessible to Canadian citizens and permanent residents.

The *Employment Manual* places a positive duty on the employment counsellors to facilitate the entry of foreign workers where the foregoing criteria are met.

7.5 THE APPLICATION PROCESS

7.5.1 WHERE TO APPLY

- The processing of an application for an employment validation generally takes place at the Canada Employment Centre in the jurisdiction in which the vacancy is located.

7.5.2 BURDEN OF PROOF ON EMPLOYER

Section 17.04(3) of the *Employment Manual* places the onus on the employer (or the employer's representative) to demonstrate that:

1. reasonable efforts to hire or train Canadian citizens and permanent residents were made;

2. qualified Canadian citizens and permanent residents were considered initially and are not available or cannot be reasonably trained for the position for which the foreign worker is requested; and/or

3. the admission that a foreign worker can create or maintain employment in Canada, provide training opportunities or transfer specialized knowledge to Canadian citizens or permanent residents or strengthen a company's competitive position in the international market place.

- Despite the facilitative aspect to the granting of Employment Validations, it is the employer's responsibility to demonstrate that the above criteria have been met in relation
  to the job offer provided to the prospective foreign employee. However, where a validation is required in order
  to obtain an employment authorization the obligations of
  the employer are limited to the aspects of the validation
  request which relate to adverse effects on Canadian citizens and permanent residents.

- It is the foreign worker's obligation to provide detailed information of her or his background and qualifications in
  order to demonstrate that she or he meets the criteria which
  the employer indicates are required in Canada at this time.

- In addition, it is the responsibility of the prospective employee to submit the employment authorization application
  to a processing post and to provide adequate information
  demonstrating that she or he meets the requirements under
  the *Act* and *Regulations* in order to enter Canada temporarily.

7.5.3 DETERMINATION OF ADVERSE EFFECTS

The determination of adverse effects, in relation to the employment of a foreign
worker on Canadian citizens and permanent residents, is based on a combination of
various factors rather than any single factor. Section 17.19 of the *Employment
Manual* states that the factors to be considered are the following:

(a) Efforts Made by Employer

- Evidence of efforts by the employer demonstrating that
  reasonable attempts have been made to hire and train
  Canadian citizens or permanent residents.

- The employer is required to demonstrate, where appropriate, evidence of advertising, consultations with unions
  or professional organizations, and the development and
  implementation of human resource planning measures that
  minimize the need for foreign workers and maximize em-

ployment opportunities for Canadian citizens and permanent residents.

(b) Availability of Canadians

In determining whether there is an availability of Canadian citizens and permanent residents to perform a task for which an employer seeks to employ a foreign worker, the CEC will consult ''reasonable sources'', which may include:

1. client inventory;

2. unemployment insurance date files;

3. labour unions and professional associations;

4. employer associations;

5. welfare offices;

6. training institutions;

7. any appropriate municipal, provincial or federal government office;

8. native Canadian bands or councils and the Human Resources Department Canada (''HRDC'') Native Coordinator;

9. HRDC Regional Labour Market Consultants; and

10. HRDC Target Group Consultants.

(c) Wages and Working Conditions

- To ensure that Canadian citizens and permanent residents are not adversely affected by the entry of foreign workers to Canada, the employer is required to establish that the wages and working conditions are both normal for the occupation and general area where the job is located, and adequate and competitive enough to attract and retain available Canadians.

199

(d) Benefits of Foreign Worker Recruitment

The employment counsellor is required to consider whether the foreign worker will have an impact in the creation or maintenance of employment opportunities for Canadian citizens or permanent residents or provide training opportunities or the transference of specialized knowledge to Canadians.

(e) Industrial Disputes

In addition to the foregoing, the employment counsellor must consider whether there is an industrial dispute in progress at the place of intended employment. If there is an industrial dispute in progress, the employment counsellor will rarely validate the job offer.

7.5.4 *BONA FIDES* OF THE JOB OFFER

The employment counsellor is required to consider whether the indicated occupational requirements for a particular occupation are *bona fide* or whether the job offer has been deliberately designed so as to be unacceptable to Canadians.

In cases where knowledge of foreign languages is required in addition to English or French, if the language is to be considered an essential and legitimate requirement of a job, the work should be of a nature that it can only performed if an employee possesses the language skills requested.

- In addition to requiring a foreign language ability, the employer would have to demonstrate that an employee would be able to assist a business to become more competitive in the international marketplace and/or result in a benefit to the community's economy. *However, knowledge of a foreign language is not sufficient in order to justify the granting of a validation.*

7.5.5 TRAINING OF CANADIANS

If Canadians cannot be trained within a reasonable period of time (normally within twelve months) and/or if the occupation is identified as an occupation where there is a designated field shortage, an offer of employment may be validated.

7.6 LEVELS OF AUTHORITY REGARDING THE GRANTING OF VALIDATIONS

The levels of authority for the validation of employment offers for foreign workers have been set out in section 17.17 of the *Employment Manual*. The levels of authority have been established in order to ensure that proper scrutiny is provided by appropriate senior employment officials in relation to the number of foreign workers to be hired by a particular employer.

The local CEC has the authority to validate up to nine offers of temporary employment for one employer. The regional offices are required to scrutinize applications where ten to forty-nine foreign workers are required in Canada. If fifty or more foreign workers are required by a particular employer, approval from national headquarters is required prior to authorizing the bulk validation request.

7.7 HIGH PROFILE CASES

Section 17.26 of the *Employment Manual* addresses the issues relating to potentially high profile foreign worker requests which are made at the CEC. Counsellors at the CEC are instructed to obtain the approval and authorization of the national headquarters (i.e., the Minister of Human Resources) in relation to the processing of such cases. The following represents a non-exhaustive list of the types of high profile foreign worker recruitment cases that quite often result in enquiries being made to the Minister:

1. managerial-administrative positions in Canadian cultural institutions (museums, concerts halls, art galleries, archives, theatres, orchestras, etc.);

2. senior positions in publicly owned institutions, corporations, etc.;

3. chief executive officers/senior executive positions with high profile Canadian corporations;

4. foreign workers destined to companies which have recently announced or are in the process of implementing layoffs; and

5. senior administrative/managerial positions in Canadian institutions of post-secondary learning (presidents, vice-presidents, bursars, registrars, or their equivalent in universities, and technical institutes, etc.)

7.8 POLICIES AND PROCEDURES FOR SPECIAL GROUPS

The *Employment Manual* contains detailed information in relation to the policies and procedures by which employment counsellors are required to consider certain

foreign worker groups such as academic, agricultural workers, auctioneers, counsellors, carnival workers, consultants/seminar leaders, entertainers, health professionals, professional engineers, religious workers, conference interpreters, persons
providing services to diplomatic missions and construction workers.

Section 17 of the *Employment Manual* provides for various policies depending on
the particular special group addressed. The "Canadians First" policy nonetheless
remains applicable in administering these group-specific policies.

Employment counsellors are guided by the objectives of general foreign worker
policies addressed earlier in this chapter. The differences which arise in the group-
specific policies and procedures vary depending on the nature and the purpose of
the foreign worker's entry to Canada.

7.9 VALIDATION APPLICATIONS/ASSESSMENT OF JOB OFFER — CEC PROCEDURES

7.9.1 ASSESSMENT OF A VALIDATION APPLICATION BY COUNSELLORS

Foreign worker requests are always assessed at the CEC (with the assistance of the
regional or national headquarters if necessary).

> • Once approval has been received and the job offer has
> been confirmed by the CEC, the employer is then in a
> position to submit an Application for Temporary Entry to
> Canada (Employment Authorization) at a processing post
> or, if appropriate, the required documents at a port of entry.

It is the responsibility of the CEC to forward the validation to the processing post
in order to allow the processing post to complete the processing of the application
for an employment authorization pertaining to the validated job offer. The employment counsellor at the CEC is required to complete an electronic form once a
decision has been made to validate the employment offer. The counsellor advising
the processing post that a job offer has been confirmed generally sends an electronic
transmission of NESS employment validation data through an on-line system. The
electronic transmission is initiated by completing the Foreign Worker Selection
Criteria Screen ("FWSC") and sending it electronically to national headquarters.
National headquarters then selects the necessary validation information from each
Regional Computer Centre which is then inserted into GEMDES which transmits
the information to the appropriate visa office. A physical document evidencing the
validation of a job offer of employment (i.e., an EMP 5056) is not required by

processing posts abroad in order to have conclusive proof that the job offer has been "officially" validated.

7.9.2 AGREEMENT BETWEEN EMPLOYER AND CANADA

Sometimes, employment counsellors may make the issuance of a validation conditional on an executed agreement between the employer and the Canadian Government. Such an agreement would normally involve an agreement by the Foreign Worker Recruitment Unit of the Canada Employment Centre to provide employment validations to a number of foreign workers for a specific period of time (usually twelve months) in exchange for the co-operation of an employer to hire a certain number of Canadian citizens or permanent residents, to promote training to a certain number of Canadian citizens and permanent residents and/or to have the foreign workers train Canadian citizens or permanent residents.

The agreement would generally contain a clause which would allow the CEC to monitor the activities of the employer in relation to the presence of the foreign worker and the ratio of Canadian citizens and permanent residents to the ratio of foreign workers at the company. The agreement may include employer reporting requirements. A copy of a sample agreement is attached as Appendix 7-A.

7.9.3 THIRD PARTY REPRESENTATION

The CEC allows third party representations. Most CEC's carefully scrutinize foreign worker requests made by third parties on behalf of an employer, and require that the representative provide the CEC with a written authorization on the employer's letterhead, signed by an authorized signing officer at the employer company.

The Foreign Recruitment Operational Guidelines, Employer Services Programs and Services Ontario Region, May 1992, provides the following directives in relation to third party requests:

CEC's must carefully scrutinize all cases where a request for a foreign worker is made through a third party, i.e.:

— the third party must provide the CEC with a written authorization on the employer's letterhead

— the CEC will contact the employer to ensure that indeed such authorization has been granted

— the CEC must be satisfied of the bona fides of the job offer before sanctioning it.

7.9.4 INFORMATION AND DOCUMENTATION INCLUDED ON THE FOREIGN WORKER REQUEST

- Generally, CECs require the employer to provide the following information in writing in order to assess a job offer:

  - Complete name, address, phone number of the business and name of contact (also place of work should the employer have more than one location).

  - Job title and complete job description, including the daily activities of the prospective employer.

  - Essential qualifications required for the position offered such as education, experience, specialized skills, certification or licensing.

  - Details of work schedule and exact wage or salary offered including any benefits or other methods of remuneration.

  - Number of employees currently employed by the company in this position.

  - Proof of the employer's recruiting efforts both internally and externally, such as copies of advertisements, resumes and names of applicants.

  - Duration of the job, whether it is a permanent or temporary position.

  - Number of employees which will be affected by the hiring of a foreign worker (*for example, the number of employees to be trained and whether anyone will be displaced/dismissed.*)

  - Long and short term benefits delivered to both the company and the local labour market by the hiring of a foreign worker such as the number of employees hired and trained and the financial benefit to the employer.

- ○ Details of the company's activities, such as type of industry, goods manufactured or description of services.

- ○ Name, complete address, date and country of birth of the foreign worker.

- In addition, CEC's generally require that the employer submit a "Foreign Worker Information Sheet" providing the following:

    1. employer/company name,

    2. foreign worker's name,

    3. mailing address,

    4. sex,

    5. country of birth,

    6. date of birth,

    7. position,

    8. duration (from — to, specific dates),

    9. job description,

    10. job requirements,

    11. salary,

    12. immigration processing location,

    13. travel information *(flight information, date of entry and departure, etc.).*

- If available, the employment counsellor may insist on obtaining a copy of the employment contract.

- Copies of any documentation indicating local recruitment activities such as advertisements for the position in local as well as national newspapers, resumes or names of applicants and reasons why Canadian citizens and permanent residents did not qualify for the particular position which the foreign worker is requested to fill should also be provided in most cases. *If this information is provided with the Foreign Worker Information Sheet and a Letter of Authorization of the third party representative handling the matter, the application package will be sufficiently detailed for an accurate assessment of the case.*

See Appendix 7-B and 7-C for copies of documentation provided by the CEC to employees and third party representatives and a sample "Foreign Worker Information Sheet" respectively.

7.10 LENGTH OF PROCESSING

Once a validation is approved, the validation information will be communicated by the National Employment Service to the immigration or visa officer by electronic message. The prospective employer will receive a letter from the CEC advising that the temporary employment validation has been sent to the immigration or visa officer.

7.10.1 EMPLOYMENT VALIDATIONS

The length of processing involved in obtaining a confirmed offer of employment from the CEC is generally between two weeks to three months. Processing time periods depend largely on the volume of work at the CEC at the time of filing the foreign worker request. There are generally three reasons for delays on an application for an employment validation:

1.   Volume of work at the CECs.

2.   The counsellor requires additional information from the employer or is required, as part of a mandate, to liaise with other governmental or non-governmental entities in order to make a determination about approving the foreign worker request. For example in the case of entertainers, the CEC is, by policy, required to liaise with unions or guilds. For foreign health practitioners, the CEC would be required to liaise with the ministries of health or departments of health of the pertinent province.

3. The number of validations sought in a particular application (i.e., where a request for a validation involves more than nine foreign workers), involves a decision by the counsellor made in conjunction with the regional office. The involvement of the regional office would, consequently, delay the decision-making process because, rather than having the CEC make the final determination directly with the employer or third party representative, the regional office would request consultation in the process and various levels of communication would be involved, including between the employer, the third party representative (if any), the CEC and a representative of the regional office.

7.10.2 EMPLOYMENT AUTHORIZATIONS

Once the validation is approved by the CEC, the validation is then forwarded to the processing post considering the Application for Temporary Entry to Canada (Employment Authorization). The length of processing of the employment authorization at the processing post depends on various factors and can normally take between one to three months and sometimes longer. The main reason for lengthier processing times at the processing post is the volume of work at a particular time.

Other factors may influence the length of processing, such as whether the particular foreign worker is required to undergo medical examinations, additional information is required from the employee in order to make a final determination that the foreign worker complies with all the requirements under the *Act* and *Regulations*, or an interview is required.

7.11 RELATIONSHIP BETWEEN CANADA EMPLOYMENT CENTRES AND PROCESSING POSTS

Upon receipt of the employment application and the approval of the validation, the immigration or visa officer is required to determine whether, indeed, the foreign worker possesses the skills for which the employer seeks her or his entry. However, it is the obligation of the processing post to ultimately decide whether the foreign worker qualifies and is, thus, eligible for temporary entry to Canada.

The determination of the suitability of the applicant's skills to the confirmed job offer involves the assessment of the *bona fides* of the application which, once again, is initially the role of the counsellor but which will, additionally, be reviewed by the immigration officer at the processing post.

As stated above, in making a determination of the application, the immigration or visa officer is required, pursuant to section 23 of the *Act*, to consult with the National Employment Service in relation to the finding of adverse effects. In other words, ultimately the decision of whether to authorize the entry of the foreign worker is that of the immigration officer handling the Application for Temporary Entry to Canada.

The responsibilities of the immigration officer at the processing post, in addition to taking into consideration the opinion of the employment counsellor, are the following:

1. Assessing the merits of the Application for Temporary Entry to Canada (Employment Authorization).

2. Reviewing the information provided by the CEC and the opinion of the employment counsellor in relation to the information provided by the applicant (i.e., foreign worker).

3. Determining whether the foreign worker is admissible to Canada pursuant to the *Act* and *Regulations* (this includes an assessment of criminal admissibility, medical admissibility, in addition to other general provisions).

4. Determining whether an interview is required.

5. Approving the Application for Temporary Entry to Canada (Employment Authorization).

6. Provision of Letter of Authorization entitling the foreign worker to apply for entry at a port of entry.

7.12 PROCEDURE FOR APPLYING FOR AN EMPLOYMENT AUTHORIZATION ONCE AN EMPLOYMENT VALIDATION IS OBTAINED

- Once the validation request is approved, the prospective employee is required to submit an application for Temporary Entry to Canada (Employment Authorization), and the following documentation:

  ○ Copy of passport (or original passport if a visitor visa is required).

  ○ Curriculum vitae detailing applicant's education and work experience.

  ○ Submission letter provided to the CEC in relation to the Foreign Worker Request unless the submission is very lengthy and includes a number of enclosures which would unduly complicate the task of the immigration officer processing the Application for Temporary Entry to Canada (Employment Authorization).

○ Letters of reference detailing work experience and work performance of the foreign worker.

○ Letter of Authorization in the event that the third party representative is submitting the Application for Temporary Entry to Canada (Employment Authorization).

○ A confirmed offer of employment received by the employer or the third party representative indicating approval of the Foreign Worker Request by the CEC.

○ Copy of employment contract or written job offer from employer describing intended position, duties, length of employment and salary.

○ Any educational diplomas or certificates, professional licence or apprenticeship papers.

○ Processing fee.

• Depending on the country of origin, other documentation may be required, however, this documentation relates to all applicants for temporary entry to Canada from particular countries of origin or place of residence and is addressed in detail in Chapter 4.

• The applicant may also be required to submit the following additional information if applicable:

○ Supplementary Information Sheet—Visitor;

○ proof of status in Canada or United States citizenship, if applicable;

○ medical examinations; and

○ information in relation to past criminal records.

- In the event that the visa officer approves the Application for Temporary Entry to Canada (Employment Authorization), the applicant will be sent a letter which authorizes her or him to apply for entry at a Canadian border crossing. The Letter of Authorization must be provided to immigration officials upon entry to Canada, at which time the inland immigration officer will issue to the applicant the required Letter of Authorization which entitles her or him to request an employment authorization at the port of entry. *The immigration officer at the Canadian port of entry has the final authority to issue the employment authorization and to allow entry into Canada.*

7.13 PROCESSING APPLICATIONS FOR EMPLOYMENT AUTHORIZATIONS AT PORT OF ENTRY OR INLAND

- Applications for temporary employment involving an employment validation, may be processed at a port of entry or from within Canada.

- The procedure for making applications at the port of entry or inland is similar. However, in the case of an inland application, the applicant would have to submit the inland application form to the Case Processing Centre in Vegreville, Alberta.

7.14 BULK VALIDATIONS

Bulk validation requests are usually made by Canadian companies which are initiating a business venture in Canada but have been quite successful in some other country prior to expanding their operation to Canada.

Bulk requests are made in anticipation of the success of the business and are made wherever more than two foreign workers are required by a given company. In the event that more than nine foreign workers are required, the regional office would have to consent to the approval of the bulk validation request. If more than forty-nine foreign workers are required, the national headquarters is required to consent to the bulk validation request.

Bulk validation requests generally involve a substantial number of foreign workers. The larger the bulk validation request, the greater the onus on the employer to prove that the entry of the foreign workers to Canada would not have an adverse effect on the employment opportunities of Canadian citizens and permanent residents.

- When submitting a bulk validation request, employers will have to provide information relating to the employees currently employed at the Canadian company and, in cases where the company is large, this may be done by dividing the categories of employees into departmental sections.

- The employer will be required to specify the total number of foreign workers required at the Canadian company as well as the classification of the foreign workers and their place in the company hierarchy.

- The following must also be specified:

  ○ the number of Canadian citizens and permanent residents on staff;

  ○ the number of foreign workers currently occupying positions at the Canadian company; and

  ○ information regarding the total number of foreign workers which will be required at the company.

- The employer should be able to identify at least one of the following benefits in relation to the entry of foreign workers to Canada:

  ○ That the Canadian company is initiating specific and well-designed training programs, prior to the departure of the foreign workers, in order to train Canadian citizens and permanent residents so that the company will not be dependent on foreign workers and to maximize the career opportunities of Canadian citizens and permanent residents.

○ That the foreign workers are necessary in order to ensure that the employer's business survives and becomes
economically competitive so as to enhance the career
opportunities of Canadian citizens and permanent residents. *In that regard, the employer will have to demonstrate that the presence of foreign workers will not only
contribute to the career opportunities of Canadian citizens and permanent residents but, in addition, will provide for training of Canadian citizens and permanent residents either through the transfer of knowledge or by
assisting the company in implementing training programs designed for Canadian citizens and permanent
residents.*

When both the CEC and the regional office, or national headquarters, are satisfied
that the bulk validation request will not have an adverse impact on the employment
opportunities of Canadian citizens and permanent residents, the bulk approval may
be authorized for the number of foreign workers requested by the employer or a
lesser number, as the case may be.

• Once the approval is received for a requested number of
foreign workers by the employer, in order to "activate" the
validations, the employer or its representative need not
provide a detailed submission in relation to the entry of
each particular foreign worker but will only have to provide
the following information for each foreign worker required:

○ Foreign Worker Information Sheet;

○ copy of the foreign worker's curriculum vitae (and, perhaps, some additional information in relation to the foreign worker's educational background and employment
qualifications); and

○ copy of the employment contract between the foreign
worker and the employer (if available).

As such, the procedure regarding the approval of each foreign worker request is
substantially simplified.

• In addition to the foregoing, there are two further documents which the CEC may require:

    ° a written human resources plan for the employer for a period of one to five years depending on the number of foreign workers requested under the bulk validation request; and

    ° a memorandum of understanding entered into between the employer and the Canada Employment and Immigration Commission addressing the labour market concerns such as:

    1. the "Canadians First" policy;

    2. non-discriminatory employment practices;

    3. the use of CEC counsellors to identify potential Canadian citizens or permanent residents able to replace foreign workers; and

    4. continued training initiatives for Canadian citizens and permanent residents so as to reduce and eliminate the need for foreign workers.

7.15 EMPLOYMENT CONTRACTS CONDITIONAL ON OBTAINING AN EMPLOYMENT VALIDATION

- Counsel should advise the prospective employer to make an offer of employment or an employment contract conditional on obtaining the necessary approvals from the CECs and Canada immigration centres and processing posts abroad. *If the employer does not make the employment agreement conditional on the receipt of an employment authorization, the employer assumes a substantial risk of liability if an employment authorization is not obtained.*

- Notwithstanding a conditional offer of employment, once the employment contract is signed by both parties, the employer is under an obligation to use "best efforts" and to do all that is reasonable under the circumstances, in order to obtain an employment validation for a foreign worker. The "best efforts" requirement applies to all conditional employment agreements regardless of whether the terms of the employment agreement actually state that the employer is required to use best efforts.

7.16 EMPLOYMENT VALIDATIONS — PERMANENT RESIDENCE VS. TEMPORARY ENTRY

Employment counsellors are generally unwilling to approve a temporary employment validation pending processing of permanent residence status involving validation.

- One practical method of solving this dual intent restriction is to submit an Application for Temporary Entry to Canada (Employment Authorization) and apply for temporary validation prior to submitting an Application for Permanent Residence in Canada.

- Once the foreign worker is in Canada, she or he may make the necessary arrangements to apply for permanent residence at a processing post abroad.

Appendix 7-A

Agreement Between:

and

Canada Employment and Immigration Commission
    4900 Yonge Street
    North York, Ontario
    M2N 6A8

In order to ensure the general public, the unions and unemployed legal residents that we are not negotiating jobs away from Canadians or Landed Immigrants; and to avoid jeopardizing your existing contracts and capital investment, an offer of employment will be validated and your foreign worker upon approval from Immigration, will be allowed to enter Canada on a temporary work permit for a period of ___ months. It is agreed this time allotment will be adequate time to train a Canadian Citizen or Permanent Resident in the skill are you have identified.

More specifically, the two parties accept and recognize the following terms and conditions:

The mandate of The Canada Employment and Immigration Commission.

That human resources planning in conjunction with business planning is the responsibility of the company. As such, the company agrees to develop and implement measures required to recruit, train, develop, and maintain its workforce in order to provide itself with a supply of local skilled workers which is adequate to meet the needs of its present and future business.

This approval is granted on the condition that during this period the company will ensure that the foreign worker train a Canadian Citizen or Permanent Resident for this position and that the company set up the necessary plan of action for the continuing training and upgrading of its local workers for its production needs, and that said worker be identified and trained in the expertise of the foreign worker and act as a back-up.

The Canada Employment Centre may monitor the activities of the worker and other recruitment and training initiatives during this period to ensure that a Canadian Citizen or Permanent Resident is being trained to meet your requirements and thus eliminate the company's future dependency on foreign workers.

Lack of evident commitment by the employer to an action strategy appropriate to local labour market conditions, and lack of progress in the employer's efforts to bring about short and long term solutions to overcome selected personnel shortages presently being experienced or expected in the future will necessitate reassessment of the situation, and could justify the Canada Employment Centre's decision to withhold the issuance of foreign worker authorizations in the future.

That employment career opportunities created be made available, firstly to employees of the respective employer and, secondly to Canadian citizens or Permanent Residents.

The issuance of this temporary validation should not be construed as a step towards permanent consideration. In fact, only in exceptional cases would a temporary permit be considered renewable. In that event, particulars regarding this request should be made available to the Canada Employment Centre as soon as possible. No request for renewal of said work permit will be considered within ___ days of its expiry date.

Upon signing of this agreement the parties understand and agree to the above terms and conditions of the approval of a "Confirmation of Offer of Employment".

System File # _____   Occupation _____

_____   _____
Canada Employment Centre   Employer

Signed in _____ this ___ day of _____

_____
Witness

Appendix 7-B

Foreign Worker Request/Assessment of Job Offer

The policy of the Federal Government is to ensure, to every possible extent, the job and career opportunities in this Country are protected for Canadians. This is commonly referred to as the **'Canadians First Policy'.** In general, Canadian employers will be authorized to recruit foreign workers (either temporary or permanent) only when it will not adversely affect employment and career opportunities of Canadians (citizens or permanent residents).

It is the responsibility of the Employer to recruit locally or nationwide for **any** job vacancy. Your Employer Counsellor will consider validation of an offer of employment for a foreign worker after thorough and extensive research has been completed. This may require several weeks or even months.

The following are examples where an employer **cannot** expect to fill a job vacancy with a foreign worker;

1. In any occupation where qualified Canadians or Permanent Residents are available, either within the local labour market or nationwide.

2. In any semi-skilled or unskilled position.

3. In any position where the Employer cannot readily prove that the foreign worker will indeed be an employee of his/her company.

4. In any scenario where the Employer does not have either an established place of business or registration number.

5. In cases where an Employer has laid off Canadians or Permanent Residences during the previous year and is now endeavouring to fill the positions with foreign workers.

6. In specialized, highly skilled, positions where the Employer cannot show how a foreign worker possessing these skills will benefit Canadians (through job creation or maintenance i.e., training)

Submissions for foreign worker recruitment must be in writing. Should you as an employer decide to retain the services of either a Lawyer or Immigration Consultant, please be advised that a letter of authorization or power of attorney must accompany this submission and be signed by yourself on your company letterhead (stationary). This authorization must specify all of the hiring activities which you have assigned to the representative.

When required, the Employment Counsellor will visit your company to give you an opportunity to both provide information or to clarify outstanding issues.

The written submission must be sent to only one Canada Employment Centre, the office which services your area. The following is a guide that will help expedite your request. Please provide the following information:

1. Complete name, address, phone number, of the business and name of contact, and place of work should you have more than one location. Also, provide your Revenue Canada Taxation number.

217

2. Job Title, complete job description and details of the job requirements such as eduction, years of work experience, specialized certificates or licences needed.

3. Details of work schedule, salary, benefits offered.

4. Number of employees currently working for you, and number of employees working for you one year ago.

5. Proof of recruiting efforts for this position, both internally (through promotion), or externally (want ads, etc.). Current human resources activities/plans with respect to recruiting for future requirements.

6. Details of the company's activities, eg. type of industry, goods manufactured, or description of services.

7. Involvement of the company in other CEIC Programs such as Work Sharing.

8. Number of foreign workers currently employed by your company, if any.

It should be noted that when examining a foreign worker proposal, the Employer Counsellor does not review the qualifications of the named foreign worker. This becomes the responsibility of an Immigration officer should validation take place. The Counsellor will explain the process to you, the employer. To this end, since the negotiations do not include the named foreign worker, the Employer Counsellor will not discuss the particulars of the submission with that individual. Furthermore, if the foreign worker whom you wish to hire is currently in Canada, his/her present Immigration status eg. work permit or visitors visa, or refugee claim will have **no bearing or influence on the final decision.** The decision to validate the offer of employment is based solely on current labour market conditions, not the foreign worker's particular desires or claims.

This Assessment is a guide only. The Employer Counsellor will contact you (or your representative) with further instructions upon receipt of a written submission.

Legal references: 1. The Unemployment Insurance Act, Part 7, Section 139(1).
                    2. Immigration Act, 1976 Section 10.
                    3. Immigration Regulations, Section 18-21.

_____, Employment Counsellor

Canada Employment Centre
416-XXX-XXXX

Canada Employment Centre
4900 Yonge Street,
North York, Ontario
A1A 1A1

6 May 1991

Dear _____

      Confirmation of Offer of Employment

For: _____

     Attached is a copy of the validation for the above foreign worker which you have required.

     This copy should be retained in your records. You may wish to send a photo-copy to the foreign worker for their information. The foreign worker should be advised to contact the Immigration office at:

             Immigration Post
             Address
             P.O. Box
             City
             Country

     The foreign worker should also be advised that contact with an Immigration Office must take place before any action (e.g., selling a property, booking a flight, etc.), since all immigration requirements must be met prior to the issuance of immigration documentation. Please note that a user fee is required by Immigration to process this request.

     Please advise this office immediately of any changes to your job offer. Any requests to extend the offer of employment **must** be received in this office at least two months prior to the expiry date on the Employment Authorization.

     If you require further information, please do not hesitate to call us at 999-9999.

               Yours truly,

               Employment Counsellor

Attach.

Canada Employment Centre
4900 Yonge Street
North York, Ontario
L4C 9T3
(416) XXX-XXXX

Dear Sir/Madam,

The Confirmation of Offer of Employment (foreign worker request) which you requested at this office regarding _____
is rejected for the reason(s) indicated below:

A _____ We have determined that qualified Canadians or Permanent Residents are available or could become available through recruiting or training measures.

B _____ There is a work slow down/lay-off in progress at your company.

C _____ The wages and/or working conditions are not adequate to attract and retain qualified Canadian Citizens or Permanent Residents.

D _____ The position is not of sufficient skill to warrant foreign worker recruitment.

E _____ The position offered to a named foreign worker is not a bona fide job vacancy.

F _____ Other: _____
_____
_____
_____

If you have any additional information which you wish us to consider, please call at your convenience.

Yours truly,

Employment Counsellor

FOREIGN WORKER REQUEST
ASSESSMENT OF JOB OFFER
GENERAL INFORMATION

The policy of the federal government is to ensure, to every possible extent, that job and career opportunities in this country are protected for Canadians. This is commonly referred to as the 'Canadians First Policy'. In general, Canadian employers will be authorized to recruit foreign workers (either temporary or permanent) only when it will not adversely effect employment and career opportunities of Canadians (citizens or permanent residents).

Generally, the only acceptable reasons for validating an employment authorization for a foreign worker are:

1) When the position is a skill shortage occupation.

2) The company will utilize the skills and expertise of the foreign worker to provide direct training for employees.

3) The foreign worker will be introducing new skills or technology into the local labour market.

4) The foreign worker will be directly responsible for creating new jobs for Canadians or Permanent Residents.

It is the responsibility of the Employer to recruit locally or nationwide for any job vacancy which a Canadian or Permanent Resident can adequately perform. In addition, for semi-skilled or unskilled positions the employer should consider training either new or existing employees. The Employment Counsellor **will not** validate an offer of employment for a foreign worker for a job vacancy in positions where a Canadian or Permanent Resident can learn the job adequately in a period of one year or less.

Should you decide to request a foreign worker, the Employment Counsellor may instruct you to provide proof of recent recruiting efforts by your company. Or, you may be required to advertise for a period of up to two months locally and nationally. Furthermore, the Employment Counsellor will only accept proof of advertisements which are deemed suitable in attracting Canadians or Permanent Residents. For example, if the going rate for a worker in the Metro Toronto labour market is $20.00 per hour, the Employer must indicate this in the ads and offer this wage to qualified Canadians or Permanent Residents. The Employment Counsellor may also advertise the position through the nationwide network of Canada Employment Centres.

Should the Employment Counsellor decide that the position cannot be readily filled through the above manner, and ultimately considers foreign worker recruitment, the Employer must not alter foreign worker. For example, in the above scenario, the employer will not be allowed to reduce the wage simply because the foreign worker is willing to work for less. The Employment Counsellor will not agree to validate an offer of employment under these conditions.

Furthermore, should the position in question require mandatory certification by a provincial or professional organization, or association/union, the Employment Counsellor may instruct your company to provide evidence from these organizations supporting foreign worker recruitment.

If your company has retained the services of a third party, eg. Lawyer or Immigration Consultant, it is required that you sign a power of attorney or letter of authorization which clearly specifies the responsibilities which you have given to your representative. You must use your company letterhead.

An assessment of a job offer to a foreign worker must contain the following information in writing:

1) Complete name, address, phone number of the business and name of contact; also place of work should you have more than one location.

2) Job Title and complete job description, including the day to day activities of the prospective worker.

3) Essential qualifications required for the position offered. eg. education, experience, specialized skills, certification or licensing etc.

4) Details of work schedule and exact wage or salary offered including any benefits or other methods or remuneration.

5) Number of employees currently employed by your company in this position.

6) Proof of your recruiting efforts, both internally and externally. eg. copies of ads and resumes, names of applicants.

7) Duration of this job, is it a permanent or temporary position?

8) Number of employees which will be affected by the hiring of a foreign worker. (e.g., how many employees to be trained. Will anyone be displaced/dismissed, etc.)

9) Long and short-term benefits derived by both the company and the local labour market by the hiring of a foreign worker. e.g., number of employees hired, trained, etc., financial benefit to the firm.

10) Details of the company's activities, e.g., type of industry, goods manufactured or description of services, etc.

11) Name, complete address, date and country of birth of the foreign worker.

This assessment is a guide only. The Employment Counsellor will base his/her decision on the information provided. The decision is based solely on labour market issues and the availability of Canadian or Permanent Resident workers. If the prospective foreign worker has any questions concerning their immigration status, advise them to contact an Immigration Officer at a Canadian Embassy, Consulate, Port of Entry or a Canada Immigration Centre.

Legal references: 1. The Unemployment Insurance Act, Part 7, Section 139(1).
                   2. Immigration Act, 1976 Section 10.
                   3. Immigration Regulations, Section 18-21.

_____

_____, Employment Counsellor

Canada Employment Centre

FOREIGN WORKER REQUEST

ASSESSMENT OF JOB OFFER

GENERAL INFORMATION

The policy of the federal government is to ensure, to every possible extent, that job and career opportunities in this country are protected for Canadians. This is commonly referred to as the **'Canadians First Policy'**. In general, Canadian employers will be authorized to recruit foreign workers (either temporary or permanent) only when it will not adversely effect employment and career opportunities of Canadians (citizens or permanent residents).

It is the responsibility of the Employer to recruit locally or nationwide for any job vacancy which a Canadian or Permanent Resident can adequately perform.

Should you decide to request a foreign worker, the Employer Counsellor may instruct you to provide proof of recent recruiting efforts by your company. Or, you may be required to advertise for a period of up to two months locally and nationally. Furthermore, the Employer Counsellor will only accept proof of advertisements which are deemed suitable in attracting Canadians or Permanent Residents. For example, if the going rate for a worker in the Metro Toronto labour market is $20.00 per hour, the Employer must indicate this in the ads and offer this wage to qualified Canadians or Permanent Residents. The Employer Counsellor may also advertise the position through the nationwide network of Canada Employment Centres.

Should the Employer Counsellor decide that the position cannot be readily filled through the above manner, and ultimately considers foreign worker recruitment, the Employer must not alter the conditions of employment, salary, qualifications etc. for a foreign worker. For example, in the above scenario, the employer will not be allowed to reduce the wage simply because the foreign worker is willing to work for less. The Employer Counsellor will not agree to sign an employment authorization under these conditions.

Furthermore, should the position in question require mandatory certification by a provincial or professional organization, or association/union, the Employer Counsellor may instruct your company to provide evidence from these organizations supporting foreign worker recruitment.

If your company has retained the services of a third party, eg. Lawyer or Immigration Consultant, it is required that you sign a power of attorney or letter of authorization which clearly specifies the responsibilities which you have given to your representative. You **must** use your company letterhead.

All requests for the recruitment of a Foreign Worker must be in writing and contain an assessment of the job offer to a foreign worker. This must contain the following information.

1) Complete name, address, phone number of the business and name of contact; also place of work should you have more than one location.

2) Job Title and complete job description, including ,the day to day activities of the prospective worker.

3) Essential qualifications required for the position offered. eg. education, experience, specialized skills, certification or licensing etc.

4) Details of work schedule and exact wage or salary offered including any benefits or other methods or remuneration.

5) Number of employees currently employed by your company in this position.

6) Proof of your recruiting efforts, both internally and externally. eg. copies of ads and resumes, names of applicants.

7) Duration of the job, is it a permanent or temporary position?

8) Number of employees which will be affected by the hiring of a foreign worker. e.g., how many employees to be trained. Will anyone be displaced/dismissed, etc.

9) Long and short-term benefits derived by both the company and the local labour market by the hiring of a foreign worker. eg. number of employees hired, trained etc., financial benefit to the firm.

10) Details of the company's activities, eg. type of industry, goods manufactured or description of services, etc.

11) Name, complete mailing address, date and country of birth of the foreign worker.

This assessment is a guide only. The Employer Counsellor will base his/her decision on the information provided. **The decision is based solely on labour market issues and the availability of Canadian or Permanent Resident workers.** If the prospective foreign worker has any questions concerning their immigration status advise them to contact a Canadian Immigration Officer at a Canadian Embassy/Consulate abroad or at a Canada Immigration Centre.

Legal references: 1. The Unemployment Insurance Act, Part 7, Section 139(1).
                       2. Immigration Act, 1976 Section 10.
                       3. Immigration Regulations, Section 18-21.

_____

_____, Employment Counsellor

Canada Employment Centre

Appendix 7-C

FOREIGN WORKER INFORMATION SHEET

EMPLOYER/COMPANY NAME:

FOREIGN WORKER'S NAME (surname first):

HOME MAILING ADDRESS:

SEX:

COUNTRY OF BIRTH:

DATE OF BIRTH:

POSITION:

DURATION (From/To - Specific Dates):

JOB DESCRIPTION:

JOB REQUIREMENT:

SALARY:

IMMIGRATION PROCESSING AT:

TRAVEL INFORMATION (flight information, Date of entry & departure etc.)

8

MISCELLANEOUS ISSUES ARISING FROM THE MIGRATION OF A FOREIGN WORKER TO CANADA

8.1 INTRODUCTION

In addition to the regulations and policies affecting the issuance of visitor visas, visitor status and employment authorizations for temporary entry, there are a number of ancillary issues which often must be addressed by applicants and/or their Canadian employers.

8.2 APPLICATION PROCESSING

- It is imperative that immigration counsel assist clients in selecting the most efficient and favourable visa/immigration office for processing of the application.

- Applicants need not apply in their home jurisdictions. They are generally free to apply at the visa office of their choice. *There are, however, a number of practical considerations in this regard. For example, applicants should generally apply to offices where they will be able to attend a personal interview if required.*

- Due to the subjective nature of various of Canada's temporary foreign worker regulations and policies, the officer assessing the application can be critical to the success of the application. *For example, one should generally be hesitant to submit applications at the port of entry without first reviewing the application with the shift supervisor of that port of entry. In most cases, the safer course of action would be to apply at a visa office which determines a sig-*

nificant number of applications in the contemplated category.

- Depending on the applicant's country of residence and intended occupation in Canada, it may be necessary for the applicant to undergo a medical examination prior to issuance of the employment authorization. *Appendix 2-D (Chapter 2) lists the countries which have been determined to have a higher risk of communicable diseases than Canada.*

  - Applicants sojourning in one or more of those countries are required to undergo medical examinations if their entry into Canada will exceed six months.

  - If the applicant's presence is urgently required and there is not sufficient time to undergo the medical examination and have the reports communicated to the visa office, it is sometimes possible for the visa officer to agree to issue a short term employment authorization valid for less than six months on condition that any subsequent extension be preceded by a completed medical report.

- Applicants from countries which are not visa exempt must obtain visitor visas prior to travelling to Canada. The visitor visa is usually obtained in conjunction with an application for employment authorization.

  - If a visa is required, the applicant will have to submit his or her original passport to the visa office rather than the photocopy at some point before the application is concluded.

  - In addition, employment authorizations cannot be made valid for longer than the validity of the applicant's passport.

  - In cases where visitor visas are required, applicants should pay the additional fee and request multiple-entry visitor visas to avoid inconvenience to the employee who likely will travel outside of Canada more than once during the validity of the employment authorization.

As stated in Chapter 6, applicants who apply at visa offices for their employment authorizations are issued a letter of authorization. This letter is presented to the Canada immigration office at a port of entry which is then responsible for printing the applicant's actual employment authorization.

- Until the actual employment authorization has been printed, the applicant is not entitled to work in Canada.

- Whenever possible, counsel should obtain a copy of the issued document from the applicant after arrival so as to confirm that its contents are accurate.

8.3 ACCOMPANYING DEPENDANTS

Frequently, temporary foreign workers are accompanied to Canada by their immediate family.

- When accompanying dependants arrive at the port of entry, it is common for them to obtain admission without documentation. This is not, however, the best method of seeking entry.

  ○ Accompanying dependants should preferably request and obtain visitor records at the port of entry which cross-reference their status to the status of the employment authorization holder. *One important purpose that this serves is that it usually means that the visitor status of the dependant will be set to expire upon the expiry of the employment authorization rather than the usual six month stay that visitors are granted. Visitor records are also required in many provinces for health coverage.*

- If the dependants are to enter Canada after the employee, the dependants should be in possession of a copy of the employee's employment authorization. *This will assist the immigration officer in the process of issuing visitor records.*

- If it is known at the time of the employee's application for an employment authorization that the dependants will be

229

accompanying the foreign worker subsequently, the identity of the accompanying dependants should be stated on the employment authorization. *This may be done by listing the dependants on the application form. Such cross-referencing will assist the officer at the port of entry who admits the dependants for entry.*

- Dependants should carry with them evidence of their relationship to the foreign worker when they arrive at the port of entry.

- Accompanying dependants should be advised that they will not be entitled to work or study in Canada merely by virtue of the fact that a member of their family holds an employment authorization.

   o Should accompanying dependants wish to work or study in Canada, they require an employment or student authorization to do so. They may apply for these documents through the Case Processing Centre in Vegreville by virtue of their status in Canada as dependants of an employment authorization holder. If it is more convenient or expeditious, they may also apply at visa offices or at the port of entry.

- If a dependant plans to attend school, the dependant should be advised not to begin school until the student authorization has been obtained. Such an application would include:

   1. the required application form;

   2. evidence of the family member's employment authorization;

   3. a photocopy of the student authorization applicant's proof of citizenship (ideally a copy of the data page of the applicant's passport or original passport if not visa exempt); and

   4. the required application fee.

    º If the application is submitted to a visa office abroad, the application must also include a letter of acceptance from the school or school board.

Sometimes, the spouse of the temporary foreign worker is not legally married to the temporary foreign worker. Canada's immigration law and regulations do not apply to common law spouses. Although Canada does not normally recognize spouses who are not legally married, as a matter of practice, common law spouses are permitted to enter Canada as visitors to accompany temporary foreign workers. Of course, it would be normal for the officer involved to satisfy herself or himself that the relationship is actually one which is akin to a common law spouse relationship and is not merely a relationship for immigration purposes.

8.4 HEALTH BENEFITS

- Applicants will, no doubt, wish to participate in the province's medicare program. Certain provinces, such as the province of Ontario, do not provide coverage in the first ninety days of arrival.

- One should determine the need for private coverage pending coverage under the provincial health plan.

- Provinces also have regulations as to whether all members of the temporary foreign worker's family are covered or merely the temporary foreign worker. *In the province of Ontario, for example, for dependants to be entitled to health coverage, it must be established that the temporary foreign worker's employment will exceed three years in Canada. This must be confirmed in writing by the employer.*

8.5 LABOUR CONTRACT ISSUES

- Counsel should advise the prospective employer to make an offer of employment or an employment contract conditional on obtaining the necessary approvals from the Canada Employment Centre and Canada Immigration processing posts.

- If the employer does not make the employment agreement conditional on the receipt of an employment authorization, the employer assumes a substantial risk of liability if one is not obtained.

Notwithstanding a conditional offer of employment, once the employment contract is signed by both parties, the employer is under an obligation to use ''best efforts'' and to do all that is reasonable under the circumstances, in order to obtain an employment authorization for a foreign worker. The ''best efforts'' requirement applies to all conditional employment agreements regardless of whether the terms of the employment agreement actually state that the employer is required to use best efforts.

8.6 CUSTOMS AND EXCISE

Temporary foreign workers who seek admission to Canada for extended periods of time often bring with them their personal effects. Such items typically include motor vehicles, household effects, plants and, from time to time, liquor and firearms. The importation of these goods is governed by the *Canada Customs Act*.

Typically, temporary foreign workers who have employment authorizations are permitted to bring most of the aforementioned items to Canada without the imposition of duty or excise tax provided that these items are not sold in Canada by the temporary foreign worker but are instead removed from Canada when the foreign worker departs from Canada. On occasion, Canada Customs may impose a bond requirement to ensure that the items are eventually removed from Canada.

Certain types of property require special considerations regarding their importation. Some of these are discussed below.

8.6.1 MOTOR VEHICLES

- Temporary foreign workers should be advised to consult with the authority which issues drivers licences in the province to which the temporary foreign worker is destined. In many cases, these licensing authorities will require temporary foreign workers to eventually obtain drivers licences from those provinces.

- Motor vehicles are not required to meet federal safety and emission standards; however, a provincial safety test might be required if the individual must license the vehicle in Canada.

8.6.2 LIQUOR AND TOBACCO

- Canada Customs has strict limitations regarding the importation of liquor and tobacco. As these limitations fluctuate from time to time, temporary foreign workers should be advised to consult with Canada Customs shortly prior to their planned entry into Canada.

There are specific provisions relating to the importation of wine collections which permit temporary foreign workers to bring with them significant quantities of liquor which might not otherwise be permitted. This often involves paying a nominal charge in terms of duties and federal and provincial taxes.

8.6.3 ITEMS FOR COMMERCIAL USE

- Foreign workers who bring in motor vehicles, farm equipment or other capital equipment for use in construction, contracting or manufacturing, or other goods for use in a trade, will be required to pay regular duties.

8.6.4 FIREARMS

Canada has strict regulations regarding the importation, regulation and use of firearms.

- Temporary foreign workers who seek to bring these weapons to Canada should be encouraged to leave them in their own country. If they are insistent on importing them into Canada, relevant licensing authorities should first be consulted.

8.6.5 PETS INCLUDING DOGS AND CATS

- Pets from the United States who are of three months or older can be brought into Canada provided that they are accompanied by certificates signed and dated by a veterinarian confirming vaccination against rabies within the last three years.

- Animal tags cannot be accepted in lieu of a certificate.

- Younger dogs and cats do not require certificates but must be in good health on arrival.

8.6.6 PLANTS

Household plants from the continental United States may enter without certificates or permits. Plants include plants commonly known as house plants, grown or intended to be grown indoors.

- Temporary foreign workers who desire to import different types of plants or plants from other jurisdictions should consult with Canada Customs. Often, in these cases, import permits would be required from Agriculture Canada.

8.6.7 LIST THE GOODS TO BE IMPORTED

- Prior to coming to Canada, temporary foreign workers should prepare a list in duplicate of all of the goods to be brought to Canada, showing the value of the goods, as well as any information regarding the make, model, and serial number where applicable.

- The list should be divided into two sections:

  o the first containing information regarding the goods that will accompany the applicants to Canada; and

  o the second containing information regarding the goods that will follow the applicants.

8.7 INCOME TAX AND PENSION ISSUES

There are many financial considerations which can arise from the movement of a temporary foreign worker to Canada. For example, Canada has a number of tax treaties which may impact on the tax payable by the temporary foreign worker while in Canada. Similarly, there are agreements relating to the transfer of pension and social security.

- Applicants who have significant financial interests in any of the above financial areas should be advised to consult appropriate legal or financial assistants. *Preferably, this advice should be sought prior to arrival in Canada so that appropriate preparations can be made to ensure that the applicant's financial dealings are structured in the most advantageous manner possible in the circumstances.*

8.8 SOCIAL INSURANCE NUMBERS

Temporary foreign workers who receive remuneration in Canada may be required to obtain a Canadian Social Insurance Number.

- It takes several weeks to obtain a Social Insurance Number. Applicants who require a Social Insurance Number should, therefore, submit their applications as soon as possible after arriving in Canada with their employment authorizations.

- Application forms may be obtained from the local Canada Employment Centre and may be submitted by mail.

Index